PROGRESSIVE VALUES

Libertarian Solutions

A Practical Guide

With a Bonus Supplement:
"Entrepreneurs in the Movies"

Gerald Schneider PhD

PAGE PUBLISHING
Conneaut Lake, PA

First originally published by Page Publishing 2022

ISBN 978-1-6624-8652-4 (pbk)
ISBN 978-1-6624-8653-1 (digital)

Printed in the United States of America

CONTENTS

INTRODUCTION

Even though libertarianism is one doctrine, every person has a different vision of it, a different emphasis in accordance with his or her special temperament and interest.

—Murray N. Rothbard (Economist, 1926–1995)

SELF-SUFFICIENT PERSONS HAVE BIRTHRIGHTS TO LIVE freely as they choose in a peaceful manner. Persons not self-sufficient, such as children and some living with disabilities, have similar birthrights subject to guidance from responsible caretakers. Peaceful means not tangibly harming innocent others or the environment on purpose except in defense absent knowable and doable peaceful alternatives. This includes property trespass, nuisance, and negligence concerns. That is what individual freedom with responsibility is. It is what libertarianism is. All else is commentary.

Birthrights are universal. Added customary and statutory rights come from different nations, tribes, and other societies. Those rights are libertarian if they do not conflict with birthrights and are generally accepted by their populations.

Individuals must also be free to voluntarily and peacefully exit communities that do not honor birthrights or embrace non-birthrights they disagree with. This includes leaving with their honestly acquired assets.

The label "liberal" is often misused in the United States. America is a liberal nation. American progressives and conservatives share common beliefs such as freedom of speech and religion, rule of law, and such. They differ mainly in their fervor about some issues. Progressives focus more on marginalized people's concerns. This includes LGBTQ inequality, immigrant xenophobia, and skin-color bigotry (colorism) among other things. Conservatives worry about faith and family values, defense of conventional behavior, and such.

Libertarian Governments

So long as government is perceived as an entity which dispenses favors to one part of society at the expense of another, it shall always be a coveted goal of power seekers to have that power… The sole function of government must be general and apply to all citizens equally.

—I. Dean Ahmad ("Libertarian Outlook," *Wheaton News*, February 10, 1983)

Libertarian governments exist by consent of the governed to secure birth and other rights individuals cannot practically safeguard themselves. Those rights are best protected by *just laws, ethical courts, police action,* and *military defense.*

Just laws are laws that do not violate birthrights and apply equally to all including government officials. No one is above or below requirements and protection of those laws. They are nondiscriminatory. Security of person, property, and voluntary contracts is guaranteed.

Ethical courts are courts that conform to the Sixth Amendment of the US Constitution:

> In all criminal prosecutions, the accused shall enjoy the right to a speedy and public trial, by an impartial jury of the state and district wherein the crime shall have been committed; which district shall have been previously ascertained by law, and to be informed of the nature and cause of the accusation; to be confronted with the witnesses against him; to have compulsory process for obtaining witnesses in his favor, and to have the assistance of counsel for his defense.

Other courts may be set up under public direction to deal with specialized civil conflicts. They include all lawsuits other than criminal proceedings.

Police action is government authority to make and enforce laws to ensure people's safety, health, and general welfare. It should not conflict with the right of individuals to protect themselves without tangibly endangering innocent others.

Military defense is government authority to maintain armed forces to defend a nation against foreign country attacks. It should only be used for necessary defense against such attacks.

Progressive Libertarian Wisdom

I tolerate with the utmost latitude the right of others to differ from me in opinion without imputing to them criminality.

—Thomas Jefferson

What is true and what is best are not necessarily the same. Truth is essentially science. It can be measured and verified by others. Deciding what is best is subjective. Human values can differ and are arguable.

Your politics depend a lot on your view of human nature. You may think people are mostly victims of circumstances they have little control over. Their intellect settled by genes, upbringing, and their environment shaped all their behavior. Faults and failures can be excused or forgiven because they did not know better. Low IQ, mental challenges, physical disabilities, dope, booze, child abuse and neglect, welfare syndrome, bigotry—you name it—explain why people misbehave. Persons who think this way might be called determinists.

Others think all people are flawed enough that they would not do what is correct on their own. They would not voluntarily give charity or help the needy unless forced to as an example. Men would not fight for their country absent a military draft. Businesses would cheat their customers unless government authority stopped them from doing so. People would run amuck; in short, given full freedom of choice. They must be coerced to what is proper. A nanny government is required to ensure fitting behavior.

These views reflect how those who embrace them think of themselves if psychologists are right. They doubt their own trustworthiness to do what is appropriate voluntarily. And so, they project those doubts on others.

Such beliefs lend themselves to support statist governments. Governments must protect persons from their worst traits. People with that view might be called Neo-Hobbesians. They follow in the tradition of seventeenth-century Enlightenment philosopher Thomas Hobbes.

Hobbes' 1651 monograph, *Leviathan*, claimed life in the original state of nature from which we emerged was "solitary, poor, nasty, brutish, and short." Monarchs were needed to keep people civilized enough to maintain a healthy society. "Who are Plato's 'philosopher kings' adequate for the task?" remains a problem for Hobbes followers.

An alternative view of human nature is that most persons—at least self-sufficient people—can control their passions and manners. They can overcome many, if not all, limits of birth, breeding, and circumstances if they choose. It is largely their choice if they do not. They themselves are essentially responsible for their actions. Those believers might be called Neo-Lockeans. Their political opinions are rooted in ideas of seventeenth-century Enlightenment philosopher John Locke.

Locke's *Essay Concerning Human Understanding* and *Two Treatises on Civil Government*, published in 1640, marked him as a leading defender of individual freedom. He surmised that life in the original state of nature from which we emerged was happy, reasoned, and tolerant. People would create and maintain civilization through natural law if left free. They only needed inalienable rights to life, liberty, and property protected by governments they had sovereignty over. The United States Declaration of Independence, Bill of Rights, and other parts of the US Constitution stem from this Lockean concept.

Libertarian thoughts on human nature also flow from Locke's philosophy although its history goes further back. Libertarians think that trust builds trust. Treat people with dignity and compassion, and they are likely to respond in kind. It brings out the best more than the worst in people in the opinion of libertarians. Their reasoning leads libertarians to not fear individual freedom. They can focus on voluntary agreements rather than government force to organize productive and peaceful societies. Rights to life, liberty, and property cannot be compromised by popularity or coercive governments for libertarians. Their thoughts about sanctity of peaceful individual freedom do not change to fit political fashions of the times. They are politically principled.

Opinions of libertarians on political issues without considering commitment to individual freedom can be misleading. Political problem solutions advanced by libertarians must be protective of individual freedom as well as practical. Practical alone is not enough. Forceful limits on peaceful personal freedom by governments for practicality if the two conflict is unacceptable to libertarians.

Sticking to political principles of individual freedom can mean tolerating peaceful behavior a libertarian dislikes or considers unhealthy. As journalist and critic, Henry Louis "HL" Mencken noted: "Standing up for freedom often means protecting a lot of sons of bitches. But what else is a true test of conviction about individual civil rights?"

Using government force rather than persuasion to end social wrong by restricting peaceful individual rights is also wrong. The common good cannot be achieved by violating those rights say libertarians. *Ends do not justify means* and *two wrongs do not make a right* are more than trite maxims to libertarians. Even democratic republics become despotic when legislative majorities crush minority freedoms. Minorities must have power to peacefully defend themselves from majority oppression by favoring laws that limit prejudicial majority legislative actions.

Individual freedom is based primarily on individual or minority rights, not majority rule, say libertarians. Power tends to corrupt and absolute power corrupts absolutely as Lord Acton famously proclaimed.

President Thomas Jefferson said, *"That government is best which governs least."* Naturalist and author, Henry David Thoreau, went even further when he noted, *"That government is best which governs not at all."*

Peaceful self-government is the best form of government for libertarians. It makes people feel good about themselves and promotes their best behavior. Power to the person becomes more important than power over others as exercised by coercive government officials.

All self-sufficient persons should be allowed to live in whatever peaceful way desired as already stated. As writer, Mark Twain, observed, *"the law is merely the opinion of politicians,"* if contrary to human rights. Those who disagree might also remember what abolitionist, Frederick Douglas, said in 1883, *"No man can put a chain about the ankle of his fellow man without at last finding the other end about his own neck."* The same holds true for persons of any sex or gender.

Libertarian philosophy even appears in the Bible: Judges 21:25 says Israel did not have a king. Instead, *"Every man did that which is right in his own eyes,"* and judges settled disputes. But Jews in Samuel 1 plead for a king. God grants their wish but warns them that a king would take their sons for his own fields, their daughters for his kitchen, their lands for his castle, and their beasts for his work. This passage provides a moral start for libertarianism. It is reflected in Thomas Paine's evidence that British royalty was not divinely endowed. This is also implied in the Magna Carta (1215). It can be seen in the Federalist Papers, calling for constitutional restraints on government. And it is found in Alex de Tocqueville's worry that even benevolent governments would overreach and disgrace citizens.

Governments often take credit for liberty they never gave. Preserving our natural freedoms has been a struggle against oppressive governments as a matter of fact. Indians, Blacks, women, and others were discriminated against at America's inception. Slavery enforced by government was wrong from the start. Protecting persons from government injustice required a Bill of Rights and other amendments to the US Constitution. It also called for civil rights acts and other courthouse decisions.

Citizen pressure should not be needed by freedom lovers to get governments to restore any birthright liberties. People should not have to fight governments to preserve freedoms they were born with. The second paragraph of the US Declaration of Independence declares, "governments are instituted" to secure rights to "life, liberty, and the pursuit of happiness." And those governments "derive their just powers from the consent of the governed." Past mistakes should not be repeated.

It is reasonable to allow societies to define themselves by peaceful individual actions. Each doing the best possible in a peaceful way translates into what societies are. The common good is best achieved this way. No philosopher kings will do it better in governments or elsewhere. Libertarianism takes the *golden rule* to its logical end.

In *Viva Zapata!*, the 1952 Hollywood film story of Emiliano Zapata, the great hero of the Mexican revolution that began in 1910 based on John Steinbeck's screenplay, Zapata (played by Marlon Brando) lectures his men as follows:

> A strong leader makes for a weak people. A strong people do not need a strong leader… About leaders. You've looked for leaders. For strong men without faults. There aren't any. There are only men like yourselves. They change, they desert, they die. There's no leader but yourselves.

This can be a libertarian mantra.

Taoism, created by Lao Tzu in the sixth century BCE, taught that individual happiness was the basis of a good society. He viewed the state with *laws and regulations more numerous than the hairs of an ox* as the constant scourge of individualism. And he opposed taxes and war. The Tao stressed self-direction, nonaggression, and voluntary exchange. That is basic to libertarianism as well as to a market economy as proposed by the Austrian school of economics.

Democracy may be better than most kinds of government. Libertarianism with peaceful control over one's personal, economic, and social activities and maximum civil rights is ideal however. The problem with democracy is that it is based on majority rule rather than minority rights. Majorities can be wrong. They get their way because they outnumber minorities who disagree. A gang of thugs can do as much.

Conventional politicians either enjoy power elections give them or fail to grasp totalitarian aspects of statism. Probably both in most instances. Handsome salaries and benefits they often get without having to account for work hours may also attract them.

What makes these politicians dangerous is their tendency toward moral relativism. Their concept of "wrong" and "right" is often clouded by "practicalities." "Situation ethics" best describes their viewpoints. They will use government force to get their way if reasoned argument and persuasion fails them.

Libertarians are frightened by willingness of many persons to automatically give authority to governments. Those citizens have not fully outgrown the need for monarchs and state "father images" to command them. They do not embrace the "spirit of 1776" and the basis of the American Revolution.

How far can societies go without the customary governments we live with? Mario Santorelli describes one such society—the Amish—in an article for the July 2004 Libertarian Party News:

> The Amish don't vote, they don't solicit for political favors, they have no lobbying group or political agendas, they don't talk politics amongst their friends inside or outside their communities, and they don't accept social security or any other form of government welfare.
>
> If the Amish need medical attention, they seek financial help within their own communities. They refuse to accept Medicare or Medicaid. They believe in only one law, the law of God as they interpret it through their version of the Bible. The Amish are indifferent to the state one way or the other.

The following public statement by the President of Eveready Machinery Company of Bridgeport, Connecticut, reported in 1983, illustrates how one individual might want to live with little government help:

> I do not choose to be a common man. It is my right to be uncommon...if I can. I seek

opportunity...not security. I do not wish to be a kept citizen, humbled and dulled by having the state look after me. I want to take the calculated risk; to dream and to build, to fail and to succeed. I refuse to barter incentive for a dole. I prefer the challenges of life to the guaranteed existence, the thrill of fulfilment to the stale calm of utopia. I will not trade freedom for beneficence nor my dignity for a handout. I will never cower before any master nor bend to any threat. It is my heritage to stand erect, proud, and unafraid; to think and act for myself; enjoy the benefits of my creations and to face the world boldly and say, this I have done. All this is what it means to be an American.

The world needs governments despite caveats here to secure birth and other rights individuals cannot safeguard themselves. That includes just laws, ethical courts, police action, and military defense as already stated. It also involves protection of Earth's environment: Land, water, air, and eco-systems not independently owned and controlled. That is the natural capital held in trust by governments for all.

How to do these things with little or no sacrifice of individual liberty is the question. That is what this book is about with emphasis on the United States of America.

Had America been a monolith…the defense of it would never have become a spiritual goal of modern humankind. Determination to stand for the United States is determination to stand for a new liberal civilization with all its multifariousness, with its "left wing" and "right wing," with its ideological and aesthetic kaleidoscope, with its hedonism and generosity…with its religious ecumenism and commercial paganism, with its bankers and tramps…preachers and muscle builders, homosexuals and wrestlers, palm readers and mathematicians, street musicians, punks, Soviet dissidents, vogue models, Chinese cooks, go-go girls and even with its real estate agents—all this enchanting marketplace! (Vasily Aksyonov, *Los Angeles Times Magazine*, June 29, 1986.)

C H A P T E R   1

Welfare

*A starving man thinks first of satisfying his hunger
before anything else. He will sell his liberty and
all for the sake of getting a morsel of food. To a
man with an empty stomach, food is God.*

—Mohandas K. Gandhi

THE ROOT OF MANY HUMAN PROBLEMS IS POVERTY. Making poor people better off will inspire them to embrace liberty and protect the environment more than otherwise. That is because liberty and environmental protection tend to be higher values that can also require subsidies. Poor people have little extra time for voluntary labor or discretionary income for subsidies. Desperately poor people are glad to survive the day let alone worry about the future or world problems.

Psychologist Abraham Maslow (1908–1970) understood this and reflected it in his *hierarchy of needs*. People could focus more on morality when basic physiological, safety, love and esteem needs were met. And liberty and environmental protection are moral values in addition to being necessary for a wholesome life. Self-actualization is the highest personal human achievement to aspire to according to Maslow.

Welfare Wisdom

> Help the poor, save the environment, discourage crime, and create a better world for all through liberty. (Mary Ruhart, *Healing Our World*)

The Sabbath and *Festival Prayer Book* used in Jewish synagogue religious services also contains a page on social responsibility. The advice given is very libertarian:

> Giving is not the essential thing, but to give with delicacy of feeling. Scripture does not say "Happy is he who giveth to the poor." But "Happy is he who wisely considereth the poor."
>
> The Kingdom of God, the rabbis held, is inconsistent with the state of social misery. They were not satisfied with merely feeding the poor. Their great ideal was to prevent poverty. They said, "Try to prevent

it by teaching men a trade. Try all methods before you permit him to become an object of charity which must degrade him, tender as your dealings with him may be."

Also, in that prayer book under social responsibility is the *Eight Degrees of Charity* by Maimonides. Maimonides, born Moses ben Maimon, was a twelfth-century rabbi, physician, and philosopher. His order of charity, one higher than the one before, is presented as follows:

> He who give grudgingly, reluctantly, or with
>> regret.
> He who gives less than he should but gives
>> graciously.
> He who gives what he should, but only after
>> he is asked.
> He who gives before he is asked
> He who gives without knowing to whom
>> he gives,
> although the recipient knows the identity
>> of the doner.
> He who gives without making his identity
>> known.

He who gives without knowing to whom
    he gives,
neither does the recipient know from whom
    he receives
He who helps a fellow man to support
    himself
by a gift, or loan, or by finding employment
    for him,
thus helping him to become self-supporting.

An often-quoted Chinese proverb says, "Give a man a fish, and you feed him for a day. Teach a man to fish, and you feed him for a lifetime." What other form of benevolence could be as great?

Charity is charity only when it is voluntarily given. It is not true charity when the giver is forced by an authority to give. Governments often use the force of taxes to provide welfare. History shows that such forced giving tends to make persons helped dependent on that welfare indefinitely. The test of a good welfare system is if it results in making welfare receivers independent.

Volunteers who aid the poor are only paid by satisfaction they get from giving such help. Contrast that to payments to government officials to manage welfare programs, academics who study the poor with public funds, nonprofit groups that use government grants to serve the needy, and doctors and health specialists whose services are called upon in government-funded poverty programs.

Government-created jobs are not assured. They can end when public subsidies run out or expire and are not renewed. That is still another weakness of dependence on government for welfare. It's better to adopt public policies that encourage independent job creation without dependence on subsidies.

Government social service workers should be rewarded based on how well they moved welfare receivers to independence. It should be left to competing charities to do the job should governments fail to obtain that independence.

Government welfare actions should not undermine or weaken attempts by independent charities to provide welfare. Welfare is best given at a subsidiarity level where givers know receivers and who truly deserves charity. Respectful appeals for charity are more likely to get voluntary charity than government mandates.

Government welfare programs can be a curse of the poor rather than their savior. It is impersonal, commonly demeaning, and often counter-productive as well as wasteful and inefficient. Post-World War II poverty in the United States fell through the 1970s as an example. This is despite government social spending averaging only 6 percent of the gross national product (GNP). Poverty has increased in the US ever since even while governments spent billions to decrease it. Something is wrong with government welfare programs whatever the excuse.

Poor inner-city residents—largely Blacks and Latinos in the US—suffer most from government welfare schemes. Moral breakdown follows not having to take more responsibility for your own welfare. Single teenage girls with shoddy education and few job prospects may be incentivized to get pregnant to qualify for government welfare benefits. Teenage boys may take little responsibility for girls they impregnate, knowing government will do the work for them.

Inner-city youths are herded into often crime-ridden government housing projects and schools that teach little. What few economic opportunities exist there outside of pimping, prostituting, drug dealing, gambling, and crime are further reduced by minimum wage and unnecessary licensing laws. Government services there, such as policing, fire protection, and garbage collecting, are usually abysmal as well.

Impoverished inner-city youths die younger and are raped, robbed, and shot by police more than their counterparts elsewhere. Getting out of the *hood* is their only hope.

Problems of poverty for single-family households headed by women are greater than ever. Fewer of these women were as poor when they lived with spouses, parents, or relatives. An unintended consequence of government household welfare aid for these women was to perpetuate their poverty. And restrictions against outside income discouraged marriage and work. It also made poor women more dependent on government help rather than personal responsibility for their welfare.

Often overlooked is the cost of government bureaucracy to administer this welfare. How much more would the poor get if welfare was given by volunteers and independent welfare organizations? Independent welfare associations believe in what they are doing. It is not just a job as it is for government agents who mostly have little direct contact with clients.

Good people deserve respect no matter their income or ability. People are not zoo animals that only need food, shelter, and restrictions on their actions. Government housing programs often treat people as if they were zoo animals. Forcing the poor to live the way government agents—keepers—want is paramount. Promoting human qualities of independent thought and action are of little or no concern.

Street people seeking a night's lodging must check into government-provided shelters by a fixed time. They usually must remain until they can be released at a certain time in the morning. Then they usually must leave the area as a concession to nearby businesses. Physical needs are met for an evening. But the price of that room and board is being locked up for the night. If they disobey the rules, they will not be allowed to return.

Government shelters can also be more dangerous than the streets. Persons who sleep there must always be on guard against harm from others. They may sleep with their shoes under bedposts to prevent shoe theft. Some street people prefer being outside and finding other ways to survive, including in winter, for safety. But they may be forced by police to seek shelter on freezing nights, like it or not.

Subsidized government housing projects are not the best answer either. As Jane Jacobs noted in her influential book years ago, *The Death and Life of Great American Cities*, these projects "become worse centers of delinquency, vandalism and general social hopelessness than the slums they were supposed to replace." Old buildings, stores, and hangouts where people interacted and watched each other disappear are replaced by blank walls and large open spaces of concrete or grass that encourage anonymity.

Affordable Housing

Better to provide more chances for voluntary free choice in housing. This can be done by zoning laws that allow for accessory apartments and boarding houses. Private bedrooms with shared bathrooms and kitchens may not be for everyone. But rents for them would likely be cheaper, affordable, and more friendly than government projects. Enforced nuisance and negligence laws can protect neighborhoods from any harm coming from those housing units.

Using *air rights* above government buildings can provide affordable housing.

Apartments built over them only require construction costs. No land purchase is needed. The units can be rented at affordable prices without any further subsidy.

What more can be done to improve the housing situation for the poor? Some suggestions follow:

- Phase out existing government projects and other housing by giving ownership to its tenants. That will cost the public less than current public subsidies from taxes.

- Ownership would move the poor tenants into the middle class at no extra public expense. Tenants can arrange whatever ownership pattern they want—condominium, cooperative, etc. Independent organizations that counsel tenants on ownership would be alerted by government officials about the phase-out. That would allow for the US Department of Housing and Urban Development to be dissolved. Ditto for local government housing agencies. These costly government bureaucracies would no longer be needed. Millions and millions of public dollars would be saved as well.

- Assure *squatters* living safely and peacefully in abandoned buildings that government authorities will not evict them. Assurance of a *home* might even encourage squatters to upgrade their living quarters through *sweat equity*. They may even want to apply for permanent ownership that turns them into ordinary owners. It should be allowed by governments. Think of it as homesteading.

- Get rid of old zoning and outdated building codes that make innovative low-cost housing hard to construct. This includes politically rather than ecologically desirable land-use density and height rules.

Ample, Cheaper, and Good Day Care

Day care is now costly to users even while paying comparatively low salaries to day-care workers. And it is not easy to find good day care providers. It makes it hard for poor single parents and caretakers to go to work without day care. Here are some ways to overcome these problems:

Allow income of day care providers to be tax free! This will be an incentive to get more day care providers to give better service at lower prices. Operators who hid their day care ventures from government officials to avoid the "tax man" could work openly. That would allow for government oversight to ensure safe day care funded by low fees from providers. The no income tax requirement and desire to work openly would discourage fee avoidance.

Government licensing does not guarantee good day care. Current standards likely reflect what the wealthy can afford instead of passable, if not fancy, safe operations. Overregulation by government can dampen would-be day care providers, using their homes to get into the business. Yet they are the ones most likely to offer economical day care.

Why assume that government agents are automatically better qualified than parents and caretakers to evaluate daycare operations? The record of government administration of its own human services institutions is far from convincing. Government inspectors armed with checklists may spot little things wrong with physical setups that parents and caretakers miss. But parents and caretakers are more likely to be thoughtful about the care children receive for the money. Government licensing also suggests approval, lulling parents and caretakers into lax personal inspection of licensed daycare facilities.

Independent accrediting groups would arise absent government licensing. They would compete on standards, offering more than one-size-fits-all government yardsticks. Parents and caretakers with any income for any level of day care would find it.

Accrediting groups will be glad to assist those unsure about what to look for.

Social Security

Retirees in the US, living on social security should not have to worry about government funding and politics. That means social security should not be dependent on taxes from a shrinking workforce. The purpose of social security is to provide financial safety for retired persons. This means it should also be sustainable. And it means not discouraging work after retirement as it does now by an earnings penalty for dollars gained above a certain amount. Better ways to ensure safe, secure, and sustainable retirement income should be considered.

One possibility is for government to phase out social security for a good alternative. Selling off surplus government-owned property and dedicating the funds to social security lump sum settlements with retirees would help. This would free them to invest the money in guaranteed accounts elsewhere, such as annuities. Younger workers could get back what they paid into social security to invest elsewhere as well.

Government social security taxes could also go into an inheritable annuity backed by US treasury bonds. That would protect the funds from political wrangle. And there would be less concern about the number of workers contributing to it. Workers with other ways to meet retirement needs should also be free to opt out of social security. This would not threaten government social security if the US treasury bond annuity idea was adopted.

An additional idea was suggested by economist Richard W. Rahn in a May 25, 2021, column in the *Washington Times*:

> One way this might be accomplished is for
> a person to have a personal tax-free free-
> dom account—like a greatly expanded IRA
> that they could draw down on whenever
> they choose or need to: for health, educa-

tion, or even a two-year vacation. The more money they put into it over a longer period, the more they would have to spend whenever and for whatever.

This would be an incentive to save as much as possible for future retirement needs!

Health Care

Governments have a duty to protect public health when individuals cannot do it peacefully, independently. That power derives from police action to secure safety, health, and general welfare as stated in the *Introduction*. But it should not be a monopoly, preventing persons from choosing better health providers should governments perform poorly. Competition allows people to know who gives good service for the money especially if not already well-informed.

Self-sufficient individuals or non-self-sufficient persons with caretaker guidance have primary responsibility for their health care. They should buy medical care insurance to cover medical expenses they would find unaffordable otherwise.

Depending on government bailouts should be a last resort so as not to be a public burden. Those unable to afford health care insurance should seek aid from charities. Such charities exist most everywhere in democratic nations with market economies. All major religions include charity in their ideology and will usually help if no one else does.

Most doctors will also find ways to serve the poor not able to pay all patient costs. And emergency rooms will treat all who need them no matter how poor.

Neo-Hobbesians (see *Introduction*) will say these medical care proposals are unrealistic. Only governments are big enough to meet medical needs of the poor.

Libertarians will think like Neo-Lockeans (see *Introduction*). They trust people in general to do the right thing when called upon. Depending more on each other than on governments for aid builds caring communities in fact. Governments caring for the poor become an excuse for individuals not to concern themselves more with the poor.

Comparative Welfare Systems

Democratic nations with market economies provide the best welfare programs. They create the wealth that allows them to afford giving welfare. Communist countries without market systems are unable to do that even if they wish to. And communist societies lack self-help and independent charities, clubs, and associations to fill in government welfare gaps.

> You should not bite the hand that feeds you.
> 'But maybe you should, if it prevents you
> from feeding yourself.' (Source Unknown)

C H A P T E R 2

The Environment

We travel together, passengers on a little spaceship, dependent on its vulnerable reserves of air and soil; all committed for our safety to its security and peace; preserved from annihilation only by the care, the work and, I will say, the love we give our fragile craft.

—Adlai E. Stevenson (Garrett Hardin,
Exploring New Ethics for Survival, 1972)

Environmental Judgments Require Balance

THE TERMS *ECOLOGY* AND *ECONOMICS* SHARE THE same Greek language roots *oikos*, meaning house or place to live. They can refer in both cases to the house we have in common: the world.

Ecology is study of the world as it exists in nature. Economics is management of the world to serve humankind. Our worldly house is best when ecology and economics are in harmony.

Almost all environmental disputes are caused by ecology and economics being out of balance. Problem solvers, planners, and politicians should take balance between the two into account when making environmental decisions.

Protecting the Commons

One role of governments is to protect the *commons*: land, water, air, life, and mineral resources held by governments in trust for all. This includes conservation, protection from pollution, land-use planning, and allowance for peaceful public use of the commons. It should not conflict with peaceful use of independently owned property not tangibly harming others or the environment. Aristotle said over 2000 years ago, "What is common to many is taken least care of, for all men have greater regard for what is their own than for what they possess in common with others."

Tragedy of the Commons

Property in government trust provides little incentive for public self-restraint in use of natural resources on properties involved. Ecologist Garrett Hardin called the dilemma "tragedy of the commons" in his 1968 essay with that title. Conservation would be the norm in contrast if these properties were owned and managed by environmental groups respectful of nature.

Government Subsidies Can Destroy Ecology

Government subsidies, such as paid-for public services, grants, and insurance, can cause ecological destruction. Such subsidies promote sprawl in rural areas where developments would ordinarily be restricted or otherwise might not come. The subsidies can also encourage unsound land-use practices that pollute land, air, and water.

Open spaces vanish in the wake of government construction of roads, water pipelines, sewers, and utilities. People would think twice before moving into undeveloped country areas absent these taxpayer-supported public amenities. Those making the move would be the few willing to live in harmony with nature with few government developments.

Building government highways to relieve auto congestion is like trying to achieve sobriety by giving drunks alcoholic drinks. It only makes matters worse in the long run. What government roadways do is pave over the countryside and invite more development, crowding, and attendant pollution.

Nature Laws

Money grants from government for state and local public works projects tend to promote ecologically destructive developments. Dams that flood open spaces are built that local citizens would never fund themselves, for example. Rivers are drowned by lakes that dams create. Places chosen for these ventures are probably where poorer people live largely and ignored by public officials. They often lack wherewithal to fight back or hire lawyers to defend them from unwanted developments.

Deserts unsuited for normal living are watered thanks to government-subsidized irrigation projects. Wetlands valuable to wildlife are drained with similar tax-paid revenues for developments. Both irrigation and drainage are done also to promote farmlands for crops often in surplus already. Scarce and precious desert and wetland natural habitats and species, along with many people, suffer as a consequence. The rich and powerful are the main beneficiaries. The meek do not inherit the Earth.

Wild areas are cleared as well for other developments using government funds. These includes areas where ecological conditions are naturally terrible for settlement absent government subsidies. Among the places are flood plains—areas next to rivers that flood periodically. Few would pick flood plains to build in without flood insurance, generally unavailable or very expensive when independently purchased. But the federal US government provides flood insurance at prices much lower than market rates. That provides an incentive for persons to live in floodplains and rebuild there after floods.

Who would move into the Southwest US if they alone paid for water needs?

Would places, such as Los Angeles or Phoenix, grow disturbingly without water and road projects funded at public expense? How about places that are regularly subject to forest fires? Who but pioneers and nature lovers would live in Alaska without government-subsidized amenities excluding oil drillers? Even uniform US postal service rates make living in remote areas artificially cheaper to live in.

Settlement would be more ecologically rational if people paid their own building and living expenses. Ecologically fragile places would be spared more often than they would with government subsidies.

American Indians

Many US national parks, forests, and recreation areas were historically taken away by government force from American Indians. Yet those places often remain of spiritual value to the tribes that originally owned them. They would protect them from development if they could. Willing tribes should be able to obtain government contracts to manage those areas for the public good. That would assure protection of those places from development while giving public access. It is worth doing since government management is subject to political change including development.

Independent Ownership Alternatives

Enlightened commercial interests, along with environmental organizations and Indian tribes, should be considered for managing the commons. Take Byron G. Norton's 1986 *Washington Post Magazine* article on exploitation of "sand dollars" as a small example.

Sand dollars are flat disklike skeletons of sea urchins with starfish designs that are often collected. The article concerned a girl of about eight, gathering sand dollars for her mom at a public beach. Her mother would bleach the sand dollars, turn them into decorative items, and sell extras to craft stores.

Norton wrote, upset by this *commercialism*, that, "No industrial operation can be expected to exercise self-restraint when there are profits to be made. The family was only transforming sand dollars into monetary dollars." He went on to say of the little girl, "As a novitiate in the order of capitalism, she was already acting as if sand dollars were merely commodities." Norton also implied that commercialism of nature leads to overharvesting of species, endangering their future survival.

But Norton is wrong! Capitalism and commercialism were not at fault for catastrophic abuse of nature in this situation. Ownership of nature and natural resources were at the root of the problem. The beach involved in his story was government *owned*. It belonged to no one and everyone as is the case with the commons. It lacked respect people give to their independently owned properties. Nature preservation would be the goal if the beach was independently owned by environmental, Indian, or similar associations.

Independent owners with commercial interest would be incentivized to prevent sand dollars from overharvest if sand dollars were a major beach attraction. It would be to the independent commercial owners' advantage to assure sustained yield of sand dollars. These owners would want to keep the public coming back for more, year after year. (Assume that there is a fee for beach usage.)

Getting beaches away from government into independent ownership by those who value sand dollars for their own or commercial sake should be the conservationists aim. Ditto for all of nature and natural resources.

The person still unconvinced about superiority of independent over government ownership of the environment should study the record. Just compare land and water bodies owned by environmental organizations to government ownership as an example. Timber and livestock interests commonly overused resources on "public" (government owned) properties without the same concern they would have for properties they independently owned.

Ecosystem Management

Ecological, economic, and social goals must be considered together when managing a biome. A biome is an integrated community of living and nonliving things. The Chesapeake Bay in the eastern United States is an example.

Forest and grass buffers around Chesapeake Bay are desirable to filter and prevent harmful land pollutants from washing into it. Much of those buffers were removed to make way for farmland to grow ethanol corn, never mind the loss of those buffers from town and city developments.

Corn requires a lot of fertilizer because it quickly exhausts soil nutrients needed for plant growth. Nitrates in fertilizer not used by the plants run into the bay. This promotes algae blooms that later decay and rob water of life-giving oxygen. That leads to needless death of bay plant and animal life. The bay is then also less welcome for fishing, boating, and other recreational and commercial uses.

It's better to maintain and increase plant buffer around the approximately 11,000 miles of bay shoreline and estuaries than growing ethanol corn there. Ideal would be a complete growing of buffers around the bay to check polluting land runoff. Working to achieve that by undoing all harm already caused by developments and farming is practically impossible. But efforts to mitigate much of that harm is doable.

A moratorium on oyster and menhaden harvesting outside of special bay farming areas until the bay is healthy again is a good start. Watermen could compete for farming areas. Losing bidders could receive compensatory payments for lost work.

Oysters left alone will filter out water pollutants. Menhaden will eat toxic algae. There are ecologically healthier places for oyster and menhaden fishing beyond that from Chesapeake Bay farmed areas.

Payments for Chesapeake renovation and watermen compensation can come from fines on polluters. This should include water supply and sewage disposal agencies. Boating, shipping, and recreational use of the bay license and user fees, buyouts of watermen, and shoreline land purchases paid for voluntarily by environmental groups, foundations, and concerned citizens rather than taxes are possible. Neo-Hobbesians (see *Introduction*) will say this is unrealistic. Neo-Lockeans (see *Introduction*) will say it should be tried first before turning to government taxes.

Waste Disposal

Government involvement in waste disposal is most often unfair, inefficient, and counter-productive as it is elsewhere. Citizen choice would make garbage more responsibly and less costly to dispose of with the environment better protected.

Waste removal by governments is unfair in part because it sacrifices some properties for others for garbage landfills. Landfill locations are more likely to go into areas where poorer, often minority, populations live. Richer people can hire lawyers to prevent landfills where they live. And they can better influence politicians through political campaign contributions to act accordingly.

Citizens opposed to garbage (commonly called "sanitary") landfills in their neighborhoods are pitted against each other at public hearings. It is a divide-and-conquer approach governments use to ensure their own power. All sides fight to gain control of government decisions on the matter. Governments win in any case by being catered to.

Governments are more entrenched and powerful than ever in the end. Citizens involved in the struggle are either beholden to or dependent on present and future government official benevolence. Might makes right as the old maxim goes. The meek do not inherit the earth.

It would be better if politics were removed from waste disposal decisions. This could only happen if governments were out of the garbage business. Individuals would be responsible for their own waste disposal. Equity and nuisance and negligence laws rather than political influence would decide where garbage goes. Governments would still be needed to enforce unmet health and safety concerns, but little else.

Waste management by governments is inefficient because it is centralized and uses sizable waste disposal and incinerator sites. Massive developments at these sites can harshly impact adjoining communities and the environment. And garbage must be transported over large areas to the sites at much extra cost and more pollution.

Independent garbage disposal sites chosen by individuals themselves will likely be smaller and more responsive to neighbor concerns. Direct costs to individuals would be an incentive to reduce their waste, repurpose it, and recycle it. Community impact would be lessened compared to government involvement. Competition from independent entrepreneurs to remove waste would be better, cheaper, and more imaginative ways for disposal.

Government waste disposal operations are counter-productive because they provide little incentive for conservation. Homeowners and businesses that recycle and conserve naturally pay as much in taxes for government garbage removal as wasteful neighbors. There is less incentive to conserve if being profligate about garbage costs no more. Each should be accountable for the waste they produce and dispose of. This is most likely when waste disposal is an individual responsibility.

Recycling

Municipal recycling does not always result in an ecology/economics balance. It may be mostly public relations. Energy required to pick up, transport, and recycle waste may not be worth the cost. Landfills that can be converted to other uses when filled may be a wiser alternative.

Some recycled products are lower in quality and more limited in what they can be used for than the same material made from virgin matter. Paper loses its strength each time it is recycled as an example. Better technology may correct such problems in the future.

Water Pollution

Silt from building and construction sites, fertilizers, animal waste, and pesticides from farms and lawns, and petroleum wastes and debris from streets are flushed into waterways. But the major water polluter in an area may be the municipal water supply and sewage disposal utility. The culprits are sewage pipe relief valves designed to reduce excess pressure on sewage lines. They routinely spill raw sewage utilities cannot handle mostly after heavy rainfalls on land hidden from sight.

Sewage pipe leaks also pollute below groundwater collection areas that provide drinking and irrigation water called aquifers. Because these utilities are generally exempt from pollution laws, they can get along without correcting the situation. Utilities should be responsible for this pollution they cause just as ordinary citizens would be. They should be fined when they do not correct the condition with money collected going to correction.

Conservation

Ecology and economics are balanced when individuals conserve; use less, make do, do without, and wear it out. It is only wrong if it seems like a sacrifice you cannot live with comfortably. A new mindset is in order in this case.

There are many sources for tips on ways to conserve. Only a few important and easy ones to do are included here.

Becoming a vegetarian is probably the best way for individuals to make a major contribution to conservation. Farm animals people eat require much land, food, and water that would be better off going to people. These animals also produce polluting wastes, along with harmful greenhouse gases from belching. A vegetarian diet is generally healthier as well. And most human pandemics have their origin in farm animals.

Ridding lawns of grass would also have a major positive impact on conservation. Grass often requires water, fertilizer, and pesticides to grow properly. It also must be mowed, which is commonly done with powered mowers that depend on polluting fossil fuels. And they make a lot of noise. Native flowers, shrubs, and trees that attract birds, bees, butterflies, and other wildlife would be a better choice. They require little or no water, and no fertilizers or pesticides.

Shower and bathe as little as possible. Normative people wash their whole body automatically whether they truly need to or not. Smelly underarms, naval, genital, and anal areas and feet can be cleaned daily with a compostable baby wipe. The rest of the body could wait on washing most often. Hair can be washed as needed under a sink faucet.

Use the blank rear of paper printed on one side from junk mail for notetaking. The draft pages for this book were written on same as an example. Return envelopes can be reused for your own mailings. Cross out existing addresses and add your own. Note on the envelope, "It pays to reuse envelopes," if you feel you must explain yourself. Paper makes up the biggest part of trash in landfills.

Wildlife and People Coexistence

Tensions arise when people move into former undeveloped places where wildlife naturally live. Three basics are needed for people and wildlife to coexist:

1. Not being overly sentimental or anthropomorphic (applying humanlike behavior) toward animals.
2. Safeguarding desirable, rare, and endangered species by protecting and enhancing their habitats.
3. Ridding homesteads of pesky and harmful wildlife and keeping land and public roads safe for people.

Controversy occurs most often when wildlife must be reduced or removed especially if it includes killing them. The conflict varies with the popularity of the wildlife involved. There are few disputes doing away with rodents that get into houses, barns, and gardens. They also carry diseases. Eliminating marauding foxes, raccoons, opossums, squirrels, skunks, and such arouse some debate. Major disagreements tend to revolve around control of selected wildlife, such as deer, wild horses, bears, geese, etc. Much of the emotion about what wildlife to protect and manage versus kill and remove is subjective.

There probably is no ideal way for people and wildlife to coexist on shared property. The best that can be hoped for is reasonable public wildlife control policy, taking all known factors into account.

End Government Subsidies for Developers

Fewer new projects that gobble up precious open space would have developers take on absent government construction of roads, utilities, and other amenities. Developers would be incentivized to build in areas with existing infrastructure if they had to pay all new development costs. That would truly produce *smart* growth. It would limit needless sprawl and better protect more natural environments within and next to urban areas.

Government land-use plans often fail because they cannot consider individual actions or predict the future. New circumstances can get people to change their minds as they age or face new problems. Those educated in ecology know there is a *spontaneous order*—checks and balances in nature from thousands of interactions between living and nonliving things. Bulldozers and large-scale government land-use plans can rarely, if ever, match spontaneous order.

Land-use mistakes by governments especially on large parcels of land can be overwhelming. They change land patterns in an area that often make corrections impossible or impractical. Individual land-use errors are mostly small-scale affairs that can be corrected or compensated for by individuals involved.

Developers seeking subsidies from governments imply doubts about their ventures. That should be enough to not risk public money by giving such subsidies. Using their own money for developments makes it more likely that the money would be used wisely. They have the most to lose if they are not sufficiently careful. The developers will suffer most rather than the public if their projects fail.

Bonds to Protect the Environment

Required posting of *assurance bonds* in advance of developments guarantees that money would be there to cover remediation costs of environmental harm caused by developments. Money involved would be put into interest-bearing escrow accounts and returned to developers less any remediation costs. Assurance bonds are also strong incentives for developers to be especially diligent in work being done. Poorer developers with good plans should be able to find enough backers to qualify for assurance bonds.

Cluster Development

Congestion is reduced, and efficiency is improved when government buildings are grouped together. Linking them to places, such as shopping centers or where public transit, is available is even better. That greatly lessens the number of trips to popular sites people often travel to. Zoning incentives can be added for developers to build more than current zoning laws allow in return for providing these government buildings. It might even include covering maintenance costs at their expense. Scattered government properties can then be sold off with the money obtained used to help balance budgets and maintain services.

New housing developments are also best clustered where infrastructure already exists, preserving open space. The idea of single-family houses on large, fenced lots must be reconsidered. Passageways for wildlife between properties to connect wildlife with food, water, and cover areas should also be taken into consideration.

Environmental Laws

Lord Acton's famous comment that power tends to corrupt and absolute power corrupts absolutely affects environmental laws. Big polluters served as advisers to the US Environmental Protection Agency (EPA) on what regulations to adopt when EPA was created in 1970. They ensured that pollution allowances could be met by their large corporations but not competitive smaller companies. That is why there are different standards for pollution on different waterways that depend on kinds of pollution. It is also true for air quality and other standards for different industries.

There should be only one standard: air in, air out; water in, water out. Quality of air and water leaving factories should at least be the same as outside air and water used. Pollution is pollution no matter how small. But giving a single deadline to all companies to meet that standard would be unrealistic and unfair. The best way for governments to enforce the standard is to meet with each polluter and jointly work out a schedule to meet the standard based on available technology and economics. Government can start with the greatest polluters and work their way down.

Environmental Justice

Special environmental courts should be created to ensure swift access and justice in lawsuits against environmentally negligent companies, developers, and polluters. Judges in these courts should be well educated in ecology and environmental laws. The courts would be funded by fines on convicted offenders and false accusers. Wealthier wrongdoers would pay extra money beyond court costs in their fines for an "environmental fund" to cover indigent felon fines. Actuaries under court direction could decide how much should be paid into the environmental fund to at least make it self-supporting. Amounts paid by the convicted would be proportional to their financial worth. No public tax money is called for.

Polluting is often cheaper than pollution prevention when pollution harm costs are paid by public funds. Fear of fines in quick-acting environmental courts would discourage polluting.

Companies that pollute can even earn extra money from government pollution relief subsidies. Here is how:

Produce things that pollute for which there is a market. Add ownership of subsidiary businesses involved in pollution clean-up. Use government loans and tax-free municipal bond money to pay for the clean-up. Companies win in three ways as a result.

Climate Change

A common error in climate change news is failure to explain the greenhouse effect. Greenhouses are glass buildings that allow sunlight in and convert it into heat that cannot escape easily. Atmospheric greenhouse gases differ in that they form a blanket around Earth that both blocks sunlight out and traps it in as heat. That greenhouse effect provides the right balance of heat for life to exist on Earth under normal conditions. Things heat up too much when unhealthy amounts of greenhouse gases are trapped in.

Venus has so much greenhouse gases in its atmosphere that it is super-hot all the time by comparison. Lack of greenhouse gases on Mars allows its surface temperatures to drop steeply below zero at night in contrast.

The unusual warming Earth is now experiencing cannot be stopped by anything known. It can be slowed by switching from fossil fuel burning to *greener* sources of energy, however. This includes solar, wind, tidal, geothermal, and nuclear energy if radiation hazards are overcome. Fossil fuels burning should be phased out as costs and technology allow. That will buy time for mitigation of and adaptation to the warming.

Nuclear Power

American government made a mistake in insuring nuclear power plants through the 1957 Price-Anderson Amendment. This amendment to the 1954 Atomic Energy Act limited nuclear power plant liability for any one accident to $560 million. Independent insurance companies refused to insure such plants at the time at normal rates because of risks involved. Government rushed nuclear power plants into production before real concerns were settled by providing insurance protection.

Risks of nuclear power plants were evident when independent insurance companies refused to insure them. Are government officials and bureaucrats better at risk assessments than independent insurance companies? Lyrics of a popular song include the observation that "fools rush in where wise men fear to tread." Governments are lobbied to help only when private special interests find it too risky to go it alone. The public takes the risk as a consequence.

Few, if any, nuclear power plants would have been built until public safety concerns were satisfied absent government insurance protection. There would be no public outcry opposed to nuclear power because of unsolved radiation and radioactive waste disposal problems. More attention would have focused earlier on solar and other clean energy sources while nuclear problems were being solved. Safe nuclear power might have evolved naturally if government stayed out of its development. But that is politics.

Fully Accounted for Environmental Costs

Some things thought to be good for the environment at first turn out to be not so good. Ethanol seemed like a fine choice initially to replace fossil fuel gasoline as an example. It could be made from renewable corn, required no dirty mining, and was less air polluting than gasoline. But not all outcomes of using ethanol were considered. Loss of land to grow food for people in favor of ethanol corn production, energy costs to produce and transport ethanol (pipelines cannot be used), and indirect harm from ethanol corn growing and use were not fully considered. This is one reason for having environmental impact statement requirements for environmental schemes.

Mandated Return-Deposits on Drink Containers

Drink container (bottle and can) deposit laws are unfair, ineffective, and counter-productive. They are biased against small businesses, only marginally help get rid of litter, and increase consumer cost. It's better that litterbugs pay for clean-up, and government taxes, regulations, and subsidies that hinder recycling be ended.

Local grocery and specialty stores are hurt the most by drink container deposit laws. These small retailers cannot afford to maintain extra space for empties or hire more help to handle them.

There is also a roach, if not a rodent problem. Roaches are attracted to residues left in empty bottles and cans. This could result in government inspectors closing shops for failure to comply with roach control regulations. Roaches at home attracted to residues left in containers stored until returned can also be a problem. Transportation for the poor and elderly to return empties to stores may also be a problem. Upfront costs for the poor may also be a negative.

Beverage prices could rise as retailers, bottlers, and producers passed along empty container handling costs to buyers. Poor people would be hurt the most by this. Container deposit laws also lull people into thinking they are doing something significant about solid waste. Not so. Only a small amount of trash is made up of bottles and cans (completely ended with municipal recycling). Most trash consists of paper products (earlier noted) that can also be recycled if clean.

Roadside litter is little reduced by container deposit laws according to studies.

The convenience of tossing away trash out windows apparently outweighs lost deposit money for many vehicle drivers. Littering is best reduced by tough and enforced anti-litter laws. Fines for littering should cover the full cost of public litter clean-up and law enforcement.

Think globally, act locally. (Attributed to architect-educator Buckminster Fuller)

CHAPTER 3

Rights

That all men are by nature equally free and independent and have certain inherent rights… Among which are the enjoyment of life and liberty, with the means of acquiring and possessing property, and pursuing and obtaining happiness and safety.

—George Mason, 1775

THERE ARE UNIVERSAL BIRTHRIGHTS AND ADDED customary and statutory rights from different societies as mentioned in the *Introduction*. Birthrights derive from the body and mind humans were born with. They are not gifts of governments or other secular authorities. Individuals can defend exclusive control over their body and mind as a result. That means individuals are responsible for what they do with their body and mind as well. This includes free will although determinists (see *Introduction*) might argue against it. Guidance from caretakers may be needed here for non-self-sufficient children and some living with disabilities also. Government laws must protect all these birthrights rather than take any away. Disputes about rights are best settled peacefully by unbiased arbitration, conflict resolution, or ethical courts.

Right to Life

The right to life is paramount. Rights have no meaning without life. That is self-evident. This becomes an issue when it comes to abortion.

Body sovereignty of mothers supersede any rights claimed for developing children in their bodies until development is complete. Development of children is most objectively complete when they leave a mother's body with the ability to live independently with caretakers. So, a mother's voluntary choice to abort is sanctioned while developing children are in her body. But governments should not pay for abortions out of respect for taxpayers who find it sinful or immoral. Governments should stay out of abortion matters altogether in fact!

Freedom of Speech

Freedom of speech against government censorship is guaranteed by the first Amendment of the US Constitution. It does not say the speech must be courteous or non-offensive. But good manners and consideration of others in speech is humane and not the same as being *politically correct*. Speech is only criminal when it tangibly endangers innocent others with no time to counter it. That is the case with the old saying about yelling fire in a crowded theater when there is none.

Sexual Rights

Justice demands that persons of any sexual orientation have the same rights under law as other citizens. Wholesome culture is built on bonds of love, personal ties, and community responsibility from all.

Marriage and lifetime partner bonds provide clean, secure, and guilt-free sexual relations. More lasting, caring, and concerned love relationships among persons of any sexual orientation should be encouraged by law. This includes property rights, inheritance rules, tax policies, and other laws now applied to heterosexual marriages.

Societies gain from lowered venereal and other diseases more likely from monogamous sexual partnerships. These bonded relationships tend to give communities stability as well that neighborhoods dominated by singles often lack.

Property Rights

Property rights are human rights with respect to property. Governments should enforce laws that protect property. This includes enforcement of pollution, trespass, nuisance, negligence, and other laws to prevent or correct harm to properties of innocent others or the environment. There should be no government limits on developments that do not tangibly injure innocent people, their properties, or the environment.

Eminent Domain Laws

Eminent domain powers prescribed by the Fifth Amendment to the US Constitution should not be abused by governments. It should be applied in a strictly limited way to land absolutely needed for public use. That changed in June 2005 when the US Supreme Court ruled 5 to 4 in *Kelo v. City of New London, Connecticut*, that private homes could be seized and turned over to *private* developers expected to pay more in taxes. Then Supreme Court Justice, Sandra Day O'Connor, wrote in dissent, "The specter of condemnation hangs over all property. Nothing is to prevent the state from replacing any Motel 6 with a Ritz Carlton, any home with a shopping mall, or any farm with a factory."

The Gazette newspaper in Montgomery County, Maryland, wrote in a February 10, 2006, editorial that:

> Once a government starts taking property
> for economic development, where does it
> end? There will always be a bigger bank
> account willing to come in and develop a
> few blocks of a revitalizing downtown area

under the guise that it would mean more in
tax receipts.

Private property owners that lose land by eminent domain are hurt if they do not agree with it. Government authorities that made decisions to seize the properties do not directly suffer. They have what in management science is called more authority than responsibility. It is unhealthy when people making eminent domain decisions do not have to live with its consequences. The same holds true for all other government-decided land use decisions.

Zoning

Zoning is a political process. It can be shaped by special interests or changed any time by governments involved. Owners should have rights to use their property in any peaceful way they choose. Peaceful means considering hazards to innocent others, nuisance and negligence concerns, civil rights, and the environment. Voluntary peaceful covenants between property owners to ensure the character of their neighborhoods without bigotry are safer alternatives. See discussion of property in chapter 2 as well.

Mansionization

"Mansionization" is the popular term for building big houses on small lots normally served by single family homes. No government actions should prevent mansionization absent measurable harm to neighbors or the environment aesthetics aside. Beauty is in the eye of the beholder as the old saying goes after all. Measurable harm would include loss in value of nearby properties, provable nuisance and negligence problems, and ecosystem havoc.

Private property is a bedrock of freedom and personal financial security. It is a human right with respect to property as already stated.

Historic Designation

Courts should decide whether a private property deserves historic designation that limits owner changes to it. That allows evidence of need for historic designation to be proven rather than being a political decision.

Immigration

Emma Lazarus was wrong about the *wretched refuse* of other nations coming to America in her famous sonnet engraved on the Statue of Liberty. The best came as they had before when government subsidies were not given. They were adventurers, entrepreneurs, hard workers, inventors, scientists, creative artists, and artisans. Some were thinkers, unafraid to peacefully break convention in pursuit of a better life. The outpouring of the best from other countries serves as an incentive for those countries to make life there better, so the best will remain.

Xenophobes are persons who have unusual fear of strangers especially foreigners. Its symptoms in the USA include prejudice against people of color from so-called *third world* nations. It is reflected past and present in immigration laws.

All immigrants except paupers and convicts could freely come to America until the Chinese Exclusion Act of 1882. Overall flow of immigrants to the US was not regulated until the Quota Law of 1924. It created the national origin system that placed visa restraints on certain nations (favoring Nordic Europeans). National origin quotas came to an end with the Immigration Act of 1965. Other immigration law proposals have come and gone ever since.

Multiethnic, not multicultural, is the correct term to describe American culture. It is not a matter of semantics. Recent immigrants may honor their heritage. But in ordinary dress and behavior, especially for their children, they are typically American. Just think of blue jeans, Disney, and McDonald's if nothing else representing usual American culture. Are there immigrant youths who do not revel in such things?

Persons have birthrights to travel to and settle in places where they can live safely and prosper unless they trespass on legal holdings of others. That gives meaning to life, liberty, and the pursuit of happiness as stated in the US Declaration of Independence. Nation-states stifle such travel through immigration laws that make governments sovereign over individuals. Worldwide respect for travel birthrights would require little need for country immigration rules in a perfect world. But the world is not perfect. Nation-states exist. As such, for self-defense, health, and safety of existing country settlers, fair immigration laws are just. Here follows just immigration guidelines that conform to libertarianism:

Your entry as an adult into this nation at official access points is welcome as long as you have no true criminal record, active catching disease (you will be directed to a treatment clinic in that instance and can apply for legal entry again when cured), have independent financial support so as not to be an unnecessary burden on government largesse, and agree to obey country laws. Children and non-self-sufficient young adults must be under the guardianship of current residents or adults that have met entry rules. Refugees will be given special consideration on a case-by-case basis.

Border protection is better achieved by fair and non-cumbersome immigration laws than barriers and walls. An assembly line that divides immigration requirements into parts staffed by specialists would make mass immigration processing speedier. That would be an incentive for honest immigrants to go through the process rather than enter the country in unauthorized ways.

Skin Color Bigotry

We need to rid ourselves of the false idea that there are races among humans. There are none biologically. Claiming and using the term race implants in people's minds that there are differences between persons based on skin color. Skin color is in fact a normal human variation just as eye and hair color are. Clear thinking involves asking why some discriminate against others because of skin color when it is just natural.

Lose the Hyphens for Americans

Americans should endorse the fact that the USA is a nation of immigrants by dropping hyphenated references to themselves. Blacks, if they wish, could call themselves Americans of African descent or heritage rather than Afro-Americans for example. Ditto for Americans from other countries. Immigrants can then better view themselves as Americans without giving up on their legacy. Others will see them more clearly as Americans as well.

Discrimination in General

Government laws that discriminate because of skin color, ethnicity, religion, sex, sexual orientation, age for adults, and disability are wrong. Nazi laws requiring German citizens to discriminate against Jews was an extreme example of government negating human rights. But personal discrimination not denying others human rights you have is fine. You are free to choose your loved ones, friends, associates, etc.

English Language

There is a dispute about making English America's official language. But English can be the official language for dealings with American governments and American government communications alone. That would be practical as well, given all the languages spoken in the USA. Singapore has four official languages but uses English alone for government business as an example. Discrimination as to what if any language other than English American governments should use would be ended. It would also be an incentive for non-English-speaking immigrants to learn English as quickly as possible.

Civil Rights of Minors

Minors living under a caretaker's roof should be subject to household rules of caretakers without tangible abuse. But when minors leave home to live on their own, they should have the same civil rights as adults. Equal justice under law means that there are no crimes applicable to minors for which adults should not be similarly answerable. Legal age defined by governments is not the same as responsible age.

American Indians

American-Indians (preferred name of late Oglala Sioux, American-Indian Movement leader, Russell Means, who thought "Native American" designation was an American colonial label) have a history of unfair and harsh treatment, to say the least, from government authorities. Dual national citizenship (tribes and US), shrinking reservation lands and Indian rights to other properties, subjection of individual Indians to the US Bureau of Indian Affairs and tribal government commands, and welfare benefits in exchange for expropriated lands make dealing with Indian civil rights complex.

Individual Indians should be free to choose their citizenship, if any. Tribes should be free to pick whatever level of autonomy they want up to complete sovereignty. All property rights should be restored, including independent ownership of reservation land. The US Bureau of Indian Affairs should be abolished, and any funds held by that agency in trust for reservation management returned to tribes involved. Tribal members should be free to choose how much and what kind of government they want, if any.

Religion

Freedom of religion depends only on making exceptions by law when its practice tangibly harms innocent people.

Civil rights include persons being free to peacefully practice their religion as they choose.

Governments should neither sponsor nor censor peaceful religious prayer in their facilities. Freedom of religion is older than the First Amendment in the Bill of Rights in the US Constitution. It is a natural or birth right that governments can only defile by legislating against it. Voluntary prayer is the expression of religious observance for most religions. This includes government (public) schools as long as such prayer is done independently without disturbing normal classroom operations.

Some claim America is a Christian nation and should honor Christian prayer in government facilities. Not so! The Tripoli Treaty of 1796 clearly says, "The government of the United States is not in any sense founded on the Christian religion."

There is no compelling reason for governments to sponsor placement of Christmas trees or other symbols of religious holidays on public property. Plenty of independent business, property owners and religious institutions do that on their own properties. Public displays on government property of religious symbols show lack of respect for symbols of other religions.

Christmas trees are not secular as many observant Christians would agree. They come from a medieval German tradition historically associated with Christmas as a Christian holiday. The public is forced to subsidize putting Christmas trees on government property, including costs of setup and lighting. This makes matters even worse for citizens who pay for but oppose government patronized religious exhibits.

Artist Rights

Government support of artists is not a good thing some think it is. Aid given is unfair, inept, and counter-productive. Subsidies for government selected artists come at the expense through taxes of other artists as well as the public. Artists who receive government funding are socially as well as financially enriched. Unfunded artists suffer accordingly. Governments should not favor some artists over others.

Worse yet, government subsidies are likely to be awarded more because of politics than merit. Artists chosen will probably be those who produce the least challenging and controversial work—not necessarily the best.

Money given by government agencies, such as the US National Endowment for the Arts, spurs dabblers to get involved. Serious artists, having enough trouble getting recognition, are made to compete for visibility with second raters. County governments are required to use national endowment money funneled to them through state governments to buy art from residents. Never mind that few if any private art patrons and connoisseurs would make such purchases.

Artists themselves become corrupted by government funding without giving it a second thought. Eager artists glad to get money from most any source line up for government grants. They make their art conform to government grant requirements no matter how much it weakens their artistic integrity.

Potential patrons make few if any individual art purchases if they are satisfied with government bought art displays. *Free* art shows (actually paid for indirectly through taxes) can be seen in government-subsidized museums. Those seeking social status from art association can gain same from activity in government-subsidized art councils. Lookers and status seekers need never buy art. They just lobby for and only support the arts through public art funding. No wonder so few good artists find private patrons! What incentive is there for more people to buy art when government provides art at no extra cost?

Art could be as much a part of most anyone's home life as are televisions, radios, and stereos. More persons would come to realize that their homes are not complete without original art furnishings. This can only happen if people learn to love art more.

And that will not occur until more individuals buy art on their own. Buying builds love. The first purchase may be difficult. But that makes later purchases easier. Art will remain the province of the elite and few until government gets out of subsidizing it.

Drug Use

A drug is a drug. Alcohol and *dope* (opiates, LSD, meth, etc.) are all drugs. Why should alcohol be legal (though usually age-restricted) and other drugs not so? Alcohol causes more harm and death than all kinds of dope combined. All drugs have real and possible bad side effects. Risks of using them should be decided by would-be users hopefully with consultation from doctors and pharmacists. Drug use should be decriminalized.

One difference between alcohol and government-declared illegal dope is that dope sales support criminals as a consequence. The same was true for alcoholic beverage use during Prohibition when use of it was illegal.

Dope selling attracts criminals because it cannot be legally bought through ordinary merchandisers. And it can be sold at high prices since dope users have no other choice. They cannot complain about it to the police because it is illegal even if the dope sold on the streets is contaminated. Children are especially in danger from street dope sales. Dope sold legally would be channeled through ethical pharmacies where parents and caretakers have a better chance of monitoring dope use by their children.

There is no guarantee that dope use by youths would drop after decriminalization. But rebellious use by young people is likely to lessen since rebellion would be less of a factor.

Crime related to dope would certainly be reduced if not ended with decriminalization. Dope would become more affordable as well as less contaminated sold through ethical pharmacies. There would be less need for crime to get money to pay for dope habits with dope more affordable. Jails would be emptied of people whose only crime was taking formerly unlawful dope. It would also check corruption of police and government officials by criminal drug dealers around the world.

Drug education would be easier with decriminalized dope use. Persons needing help with dope habits could openly ask for aid without being jailed or labeled a criminal.

In no way should government encourage use of dope by declaring it legal rather than decriminalized. This is more than a semantic difference. Legalization can be mistaken as an endorsement by governments of dope use. Let adults decide for themselves how to deal with dope use as they do with alcohol or cigarettes. Non-self-sufficient children and adults would still need guidance from parents, caretakers, and the health community voluntarily.

Affirmative Action

Affirmative action is good when implemented independently to make up for past injustices that harmed minorities. Not so when done by government. That is because equal justice under law should mean only one category of citizen with the same rights. Certain groups have been historically unfairly treated by government. This includes people of color in addition to slaves, American-Indians, and persons of some religions. But that does not mean innocent people should be forced by government to pay for those wrongs.

To call government affirmative action civil rights is revisionism at its worst. Even ordinary dictionaries include guarantees of equal treatment under law in their definitions of civil rights. Giving some citizens preference over others by government legislation violates the equal treatment civil rights idea. Paraphrasing author George Orwell's famous dictum in his *Animal Farm* novel, "All people are equal, but some are more equal than others. That is what government authorities say to all citizens when it uses affirmative action to correct past civil abuses."

It is sad to see persons historically oppressed seek to be oppressors themselves. For them to ruthlessly use government to suppress legal even with unsavory ideas of opponents is especially repugnant. Civil rights cannot be situational. It is all or nothing!

There is a need for diversity in institutions, however. Choosing people of color or anyone else not well represented for diversity is fine. It is the proper alternative to affirmative action!

Firearms

Author George Orwell of 1984 fame wrote in his *Essays, Volume IV*,

> Though I have no doubt exceptions can be
> brought forward, I think the following rule
> would be found generally true: that in ages
> in which the dominant weapon is cheap
> and simple, the common people will have
> a chance...

Firearms fit that description! Most look only at harm firearms do in the hands of criminals or terrorists and in careless accidents.

Few focus on firearms as a deterrent against crime and use in defense. Skills in martial arms or use of sharp objects like swords in defense require much training and expertise. Shooting firearms just involves aiming and pulling a trigger and is relatively easy to master. And simple firearms are not expensive.

Face it. People who want government-enforced firearms control are fearful of or prejudiced against firearms and their owners. Firearms like knives, clubs, vehicles, etc. are inert objects. They do not cause harm by themselves unless people choose to use them that way. It is people who harm and kill others and will use any convenient objects to do so. Laws limiting firearms ownership by innocent persons ensures that law-disobeying offenders alone will have firearms.

Those wanting government-enforced firearms control are dangerous! They reject facts to the contrary having already decided that firearms are inherently evil. They would deny ordinary citizens from owning firearms for the doubtful possibility of saving some innocent lives. These tend to be the same people who use force of government instead of friendly persuasion through arguments to impose their will on others. Some have the nerve to call themselves liberals or progressives!

Firearms are especially important to some persons, such as women, the poor, and the elderly for defense. Just flashing a firearm can deter rapes, muggings, and burglaries. Even the so-called Saturday night specials will frighten criminals away. These cheap firearms are often the choice of poor people most likely to be victimized and least able to purchase more costly firearms.

Those lobbying for government firearms control assume free countries will always be that way. So, they have no trouble with firearm control laws in those nations. Just imagine what formerly free countries that become totalitarian would do with firearm ownership records. Nazi Germany was a prime example (see Stephen P. Halbrook's book, *Gun Control in the Third Reich*).

Firearms might have been the only thing that prevented government sheriffs and police from murdering blacks in the

USA not so very long ago. And government police may not respond even if called for to some crime-infested areas (often inner-city neighborhoods). How are innocent people stuck in these places supposed to protect themselves without firearms?

Not everyone is comfortable owning firearms. But firearms should be available to innocent citizens with no government hassle.

Businesses

Businesspeople have the same personal human rights as everyone else. But dealing with the public means entering the commons and having to abide by community laws and standards. It includes not discriminating against employees, customers, and suppliers based on their physical characteristics.

Governments tend to control businesses for the political common good when businesses fail to fully account for externalities. Externalities include land, air, and water resource uses that affect employees, customers, suppliers, and the environment.

Government business regulation would be less sought after if business model bookkeeping fully accounted for these externality costs.

Government policies should encourage rather than stifle entrepreneurial business creation and jobs that go with it. Entrepreneurs generally hate people looking over their shoulders and telling them what to do. Better for governments to provide entrepreneurs with incentives to expand present day enterprises and invent fresh businesses. It involves freedom from *needless* taxes and government regulation.

User fees and bonds can take the place of taxes for most services only governments can provide (see chapter 7). Criminal and civil law can keep entrepreneurs honest and wholesome. Competition and consumer education will promote making products and services superior and cheaper. Insurance and banking requirements foster prudent business decision-making. Government agencies subject to politics are less able to be objective about control over entrepreneur activities.

It is common knowledge that independent businesses usually can conduct money-making enterprises better than government can. Government-run businesses tend to cost too much, lose money, give poor service, and waste assets. Politics often intrude. And government-run businesses are not subject to taxes, legal restraints, rules, and regulations required of independent businesses. There is little reason for governments to engage in any real or money-making venture independently available in fact. Economic fascism exists when independent businesses are so government regulated that those governments dictate almost all business operations.

Businesses free to compete without government and/or protection can only achieve monopoly status if they earn it. Such monopolies become same when offering quality goods and services at competitive prices competition cannot match.

Government licensing of professions and businesses is often based on politics more than fitness of recipients. Requirements for licenses are usually determined by those already licensed. They are commonly designed to reduce competition. Current license holders are *grandfathered* in when licensing standards are adopted, so they need not meet them. The main purpose for licensing is to increase government revenues through license fees in any case.

Licensing of businesses is best left to independent groups offering certifications. Independent certifying organizations would compete to get consumers to do business with professionals and businesses they certify. Competing certifying associations would raise standards and offer more choices in trying to outdo each other. Consumers would benefit instead of being stuck with a single government standard as they are now.

Some businesses think money is money whether it comes from governments or not. They willingly surrender power to governments in return for favors, subsidies, and protection from competition. Partnerships between governments and favored businesses at the expense of competing businesses is unfair crony capitalism. It justifies government power to rule businesses as well and moves America further into economic fascism.

Business Districts

It is best to give businesses in concentrated business areas as much control of their streets and parking areas as possible. They should pay the costs of maintenance and security of these places in return. That would be an incentive for businesses to keep business areas clean and safe day and night. Tax credits can also be given as a reward for not making those business areas more of a public expense. Any management by businesses can not violate civil rights of users in those areas, however.

Business Affirmative Action

Many minority business owners have been discriminated against historically.

That does not mean minority-owned businesses should categorically be given preference in awards of government contracts over competing businesses. Such discrimination should be examined on a case-by-case basis and dealt with accordingly if at all. Minority businesspeople can only get preference by discriminating against nonminority businesspersons. One unfairness should not be corrected by another unfairness. What government officials should ask themselves is why more minority-owned businesses fail to get contracts without special consideration?

Constantly telling minorities they cannot succeed without special government help undermines self-respect. It can become a self-fulfilling prophecy, leading minorities in the wrong direction to get the success they deserve. Economist Thomas Sowell in his book, *Civil Rights: Rhetoric or Reality*, writes:

> …among the insidious dangers are the undermining of minority and female self-confidence by incessant reiteration of the themes of pervasive discrimination, hypercritical standards and shadowy but malign enemies relentlessly opposing their progress…it obscures the urgency of acquiring the attitudes to apply them with best results. Pride of achievement is also undermined by the civil rights vision that assumes credit for minority and female advancement. This makes minority and female achievement suspect in their own eyes and in the eyes of the larger society.

Unions

Nongovernment employee unions paved the way for worker protections in early years of the twentieth century.

Their decline began with passage of the 1935 National Labor Relations Act (NLRA).

The NLRA promoted use of government force rather than peaceful voluntary worker negotiations for concessions directly with employers. That power led to union greed, and the combination of government power and union greed bred union corruption. Union self-interest rather than the common good became supreme. It would be best to repeal the NLRA and abolish the NLR Board.

Contrast this with the philosophy of the father of American unionism, Samuel Gompers. Written on his monument in Samuel Gompers Memorial Park in Washington, DC, are the following quotes:

> No lasting gain ever came by compulsion. If we seek force, we tear apart that which, united, is invincible. There is no way whereby our labor movement may be assured sustained progress in determining its policies and its plans other than sincere democratic deliberation until a unanimous decision is reached. This may seem a cumbrous, slow method to the impatient, but the impatient are more concerned for immediate triumph than for the education of constructive development.

So long as we hold fast to voluntary principles and have been actuated and inspired by the spirit of service, we have sustained our forward progress and we have made our labor movement something to be respected and accorded a place in the councils of our republic. Where we have blundered into trying to force a policy or a decision, even though wise and right, we have impeded if not interrupted the realization of our aims.

Equal Employment Laws

Equal employment laws may seem fair and benign at first glance. But they invite abuse. Workers not hired or promoted, or who are fired for incompetence might falsely blame the action on discrimination. It is an easy charge to make and a difficult charge to defend against. Employers unfortunately remain suspect even when discrimination charges are dismissed in court. Better to encourage conflict resolution on a case-by-case basis.

Employers are emboldened by equal employment laws to discriminate in employment to avoid potential public relations problems. Minority quotas are adopted unofficially just to play it safe even at the expense of innocent workers.

Day Labor Centers

Day labor centers need to be set up in a way that respects contractors, workers, and the public. That includes limits on contractors to exploit laborers and vice-versa without public subsidy. Sponsorship of day labor centers should be done by business and labor organizations independent of government.

One way is to have dispatchers at day labor centers register contractors and get them to fill in preprinted forms, agreeing to work and wage rates for laborers. A fee would be charged, shared by contractors and workers to make day labor center costs self-supporting. Dispatchers would then link contractors with laborers. Workers could be registered by code numbers without the need to show identity for security reasons. This procedure need only be done once for repeat contractors and laborers. It would not be a bureaucratic or time-consuming venture. Follow-up in case of cheating would be easier to detect and correct. And privacy would be protected.

Minimum Wage Laws

Minimum wage laws encourage employers to hire more skilled adults over unskilled teenagers or turn to robotics. Small businesses may even be forced to close if salary demands of employees are too high to support. That means fewer jobs available since most of them are created by small businesses.

High teenage unemployment generates desperation that can translate into crimes for teens to get money.

Government Citizen Surveillance

Late US Supreme Court Justice, Louis Brandeis, said privacy rights were the most valued right of civilized people. It is codified in the Fourth Amendment of the US Constitution, which reads as follows:

> The right of the people to be secure in their persons, houses, papers and effects, against unreasonable searches and seizures, shall not be violated, and no warrants shall issue, but upon probable cause, supported by Oath or affirmation, and particularly describing the place to be searched, and the person or things to be seized.

This right has historically been abused by the US government and not honored at all by totalitarian governments. The Federal Bureau of Investigation (FBI) has done this because of ideology and politics rather than criminal wrongdoing. Their *Domestic Investigations and Operations Guide* updated in 2016 allows them to investigate individuals and groups with no evidence of law-breaking. All they need is an *authorized purpose* and a distinct objective. That means being allowed to investigate persons and organizations without probable cause or search warrants. The US Congress and courts have not done their duty their constitutional oath requires to check these abuses.

The Foreign Intelligence Surveillance Act (FISA) passed by the US Congress in 1979 requires government to obtain a warrant from a secret court of judges appointed by the Chief Justice of the United States to conduct domestic espionage. Surveillance of *aliens* abroad has always been and remains legal. US presidents have been able to bypass FISA by claiming that the Authorization for Use of Military Force (AUMF) action passed by Congress September 2001 allows them to ignore FISA. AUMF permits presidents

> to use all necessary and appropriate force against those nations, organizations, or persons he determines planned, authorized, or aided the terrorist attacks that occurred on September 11, 2001, or harbored such organizations or persons, in order to prevent any future acts of international terrorism against the United States by such nations, organizations, or persons.

The Patriot Act passed by Congress in October 2001 is a wide-ranging (342 pages long) anti-terrorism law that has since been renewed with few changes. This law is a threat to basic First and Fourth Amendment rights to free speech and privacy. It strengthened the Bank Secrecy Act that requires financial institutions (creditors and gambling casinos in addition to banks) to report to the US Treasury Department any financial transactions that these institutions find out of the ordinary through a Suspicious Activity Report (SAR). Suspicious transactions include making unusually large money deposits. It is illegal for a financial institution to tell consumers that an SAR has been filed on them. This is an invasion of privacy that does not really provide anti-terrorism protection.

The constitutional separation of power (judicial review) is violated when a president allows the National Security Agency (NSA) to conduct domestic surveillance without FISA limitations. James Madison said in 1788 that he believes "there are more instances of the abridgement of freedom of people by gradual and silent encroachment of those in power than by violent and sudden usurpations." William Pitt said in 1783, "Necessity is the plea for every infringement of human freedom. It is the argument of tyrants. It is the creed of slaves."

Congress should cancel FISA, AUMF, and the Patriot Act to help restore individual rights. It should also stop NSA from conducting general domestic surveillance. What follows is a song about NSA.

"The NSA May Be Bugging Your Phone"
(Sung to the tune of "Santa Claus
Is Coming to Town." Original lyrics
by Gerald Schneider, Ph.D.)

You better watch out, better not cry,

"Secret spying," I'm telling you why.

The NSA may be bugging your phone.

They're making a list, checking it twice,

To see if your "left", or not quite "right,"

The NSA may be bugging your phone.

They listen and they're peeping,

They watch for a mistake,

They know if you hate Democrats,

Or Republicans for goodness' sake.

Oh, you better watch out, better not complain,

It may be illegal, they'll do it just the same,

The NSA may be bugging your phone.

Protecting Our Rights Against "But-Heads"

Democracy does not guarantee liberty. Think of nations where dictatorial governments were elected by majority rule. Thirst for democracy in any event must come from within. It rarely, if ever, can be imposed by outside force of arms. Freedom occurs when individual rights are respected. So why is it a constant struggle to protect against limits of those rights by "*but*-heads?"

You know who they are. They are persons who claim belief in unalienable individual rights to life, liberty, and pursuit of happiness, *but*. There are always qualifications on those birthrights through use of the word *but* that reveal hypocrisy in their constructs. Some examples:

They believe in freedom of speech *but* exclude speech they hate. They believe in freedom of association, *but* support laws that discriminate against peaceful groups they do not like. They believe in the Constitution's Bill of Rights, *but* not certain rights included, such as the Second Amendment. They believe in personal rights over your body when not harming others, *but* not what you drink or smoke.

In short, they believe whatever legislators do that they like trumps unalienable birthrights, "*But*-heads" must not gain more power from government to force restrictions on individual birthrights.

Relying on Government Wisdom

It is important to remind ourselves that politicians we elect to office are not gods! They make mistakes as we all do. You cannot safely depend on them to know what is right for the nation. Your conscience must remain the guideline for your thoughts on what is best for the country. But you must hold yourself accountable for actions you take because of your conscience. This includes holding yourself responsible for existing laws you violate if any because of conscientious objection.

> Experience should teach us to be most on our guard to protect liberty when the government's purposes are beneficent. Men born to freedom are naturally alert to repel invasion of their liberty by evil-minded rulers. The greatest dangers to liberty lurk in insidious encroachment by men of zeal, well-meaning but without understanding. (Louis D. Brandeis, in a dissenting US Supreme Court opinion, *Olmstead v. United States*, 1928)

C H A P T E R   4

Defense without Offense

We have become a nation of nuclear giants and ethical
infants. We know more about war than we do about
peace, more about killing than we do about living.

—Gen. Omar Bradley (1893–1981)

WORLD PEACE DEPENDS IN PART ON ALL GOV-
ernments demanding the same morality for
themselves as for their citizens. There should
be no double-standard for morality: one for government,
and one for individual citizens. Government should *not* have
power to steal, cheat, commit fraud, or tangibly harm innocent people. Ends do not justify means even if government
officials claim so for protection or in the public interest. This
includes giving comfort and support to foreign dictators who
violate human rights.

Nothing moral can be achieved by immoral means. Weapons cannot bring peace and safety if individual human rights are sacrificed supposedly to attain security.

Military Defense

Two insights guide thoughts about defense without offense. First, the more defense nations provide other nations, the less aided nations take responsibility for their own defense. Second, absent outside help, countries with the most at stake in conflicts are incentivized to seek peace. George Washington came close to that when he said, "The great rule in conduct for us, in regard to foreign nations, is in extending our commercial relations to have with them as little political connection as possible." Thomas Jefferson reinforced Washington when he said, "Peace, commerce, and honest friendship with all nations—entangling alliances with none." Both fell a little short in their statements by not saying more about countries that *flagrantly* violate human rights. No nation is perfect on this account.

Next step to American peace is withdrawal from NATO. Europe is rich enough to take care of itself. Ditto for Japan, South Korea, and most other countries America provides military support to.

Foreign policy should embrace free trade and friendship without support for human rights abuses by foreign governments. Human rights misdeeds should be countered by peaceful suasion, censure, and international court actions. Brains instead of bullets!

Government aid to other nations should only be given in humanitarian emergencies when they honestly cannot provide it themselves. The best aid is voluntary that goes directly to needy individuals and independent aid organizations, and promotes self-sufficiency. Government-to-government help often ends up in the hands of gangs or Swiss bank accounts rather than the stricken.

Nation-state military defense without offense should follow an Avoid, Deter, Defend (ADD) approach in that order:

First, *avoid* starting fights with other countries. Focus should be on peaceful conflict resolution against hostile actions by other nations. Promote, lead, and enter into monitored arms-reduction treaties, including phase-out of chemical, biological, and radiological weapons. Make no defense pacts with foreign nations except when necessary to defend against a looming attack on your country. Keep no soldiers or build and maintain military installations in foreign nations when at peace. Look for common ground for working together for peace with other countries, regardless of how they are governed. But do not overlook human rights concerns as previously noted.

Second, *deter* attacks from foreign nations if they cannot be avoided. This means power to defend against all military assaults from land, sea, air, and space with conventional weapons. Defense against cyber-attacks included. It should be enough to convince unfriendly countries and terrorist groups that any warlike attack would be futile.

Third, *defend* militarily against foreign nation assaults that cannot be deterred absent any knowable or possible peaceful choice. War should truly be a last resort. Ideal weapons should impede or prevent enemy actions with minimal death, property destruction, pollution, or harm to innocents. Military costs should be funded as much as possible from a national military lottery, defense bonds, and voluntary donations. US military bases around the world could be sold off and soldiers there brought home to fulfill military quotas. Money could be saved by ending US subsidies for other nations' militaries. This includes NATO already mentioned.

Anti-War Protests

It is good for people to be involved in peaceful anti-war protests. But they should be well-informed when they do. Propaganda is no substitute for reasoned arguments. And mindless hate, name calling, innuendo, and incivility will not change viewpoints of those who disagree with you. It will only encourage them to dismiss you as an unthinking malcontent.

Free Trade and Commerce

Free trade and commerce provide links between buyers and sellers that encourages peace to avoid losses by war. It is true for individuals and nations that do not like each other as well. Foreign sellers have little incentive to kill American buyers and vice versa as an example.

A Military Draft

There should not be a military draft registration in times of peace (when not at war). Such registration is a form of involuntary servitude to the state. It makes it easier for a nation to go to war even when such wars are unpopular, undeclared by legislation, and truly optional. A free society should not compel the young into military service against their will unless absolutely necessary.

The American Revolutionary and War of 1812 had enough American citizen support so that a draft was not necessary. The Korean and Vietnam wars would not have happened without a draft because they lacked widespread citizen support. It proves that citizens will voluntarily support wars *when necessary* for self-defense! But they will not voluntarily fight wars when the aggressor is their own nation. That better ensures peaceful relations with other countries unless they militarily attack yours.

Involuntary servitude was outlawed by the Thirteenth Amendment to the US Constitution. It should certainly prohibit government forcing citizens against their will from serving the state as a draft does. Daniel Webster said the following in the US Congress in connection with proposed draft legislation in 1814,

> Where is it written in the Constitution that you may take children from their parents, and parents from their children, and compel them to fight the battles of any war, in which the folly and wickedness of Government engage it?

American tradition is based on patriotic citizen soldiers who fight for country to protect it from tyranny voluntarily. One should be suspicious of wars (*military conflicts* when not legally declared by Congress) that lack sufficient voluntary citizen support. *Force* is used by governments when they fail to convince enough citizens of merits of something by argument.

Draft registration is not efficient or effective anyway. Young people who register for a draft tend to move without telling authorities of address changes. Call-ups would be difficult at best. And how many soldiers in combat would choose to depend on other soldiers who do not want to be there?

In his 1970 Libertarian presidential campaign book, *Liberty Reclaimed: A New Look at American Politics*, Jim Lewis wrote:

> The first successful attempt at consolidating political power in the hands of the federal government came with the election of Lincoln and the Civil War. The writ of habeus corpus was suspended by Lincoln, political opponents were arrested, opposition newspapers were shut down by federal troops, a draft was instituted, greater tariffs were passed as was an income tax. The war served as an excuse for massive expansion of federal power. This is one reason why true advocates of a free economy have always been advocates of pro-peace foreign policies.
>
> There is no difference in *principle* between the black slave in 1860 and the national service draftee in 1970. Both are cases of involuntary servitude.

Government Intelligence Activities

Antidemocratic intelligence activities by government should be ended. This includes covert actions by civilian government intelligence agencies. Covert actions should occur only when militarily necessary under military authorities authorized by Congress through the President.

Covert actions are secret intelligence programs to further foreign policy aims as construed by government authorities. Involved are selected foreign government political support projects, propaganda campaigns, and paramilitary operations. They encourage government agents to lie, cheat, and maybe murder without due process. And their hidden nature makes government officials less accountable to Americans for actions taken. This should not happen outside the military in times of war.

Corruption results from manipulation of data and conclusions that make them conform to current political views and policies. Recall illegal Iran-Contra activities and secret US wars in Guatemala, Cuba, Chile, Burma, Namibia, Angola, the Middle-East, and elsewhere. Also, low enemy strength figures reported to Americans to maintain support for the Vietnam War.

Secret foreign policy, covert actions, and spying are not needed to protect from real or imagined enemies. Knowledge of US military might should be sufficient to deter attacks by foreign powers. Countries lose respect from and influence on foreign nations without open and honest dealings with them. Nations also gain morally by conducting foreign policy publicly. Why should any person of integrity fear frank and truthful political activity?

The Soviet Union was the main target of the 1947 US National Security Act that encouraged modern covert actions. It should be repealed for a better law that ensures no government civilian covert actions.

Even advocates of continued US government intelligence work admit that intelligence activities bog down in bureaucracy. Slowness to act, changes in administrations, too narrow assignments on a need-to-know basis, and influx of more data than can be properly evaluated lead to ineptness and inefficiency. Recall the failure of American intelligence agencies about *weapons of mass destruction* in Iraq that led us into war with Iraq. And was America's twenty-year war with Afghanistan really necessary?

Nuclear Weapons

Nuclear weapons should be banned! They are inherently offensive since they cannot be targeted against attackers without radiation fallout spreading elsewhere. That harms innocent people needlessly and the environment worldwide for years. Contrast that to firearms, knives, swords, arrows, etc. that can pinpoint enemies even when mixed with friendly force without fallout. And now we have drones and cyber weapons.

Conventional weapons can be used to destroy incoming missiles for defense. The US army was the first to demonstrate this June 10, 1984. They destroyed an incoming ballistic missile warhead with a nonnuclear ABM (antiballistic missile) more than 100 miles above the Western Pacific Ocean. Much better conventional deterrent weapons have been developed since.

Another peace move for America would be to dismantle its entire land-based missile defense system. That would still leave an ample mobile bomber and atomic submarine counter-force power for defense. It would also ensure that the US mainland is not a crucial military target. That would make Americans even safer than ever from a first-strike missile assault.

The Treaty of the Non-Proliferation of nuclear weapons (NPT) was signed in 1968 by 191 nations. It included the five countries with nuclear bombs then—the US, Soviet Union, United Kingdom, France, and China. India, Pakistan, and North Korea developed a nuclear weapon arsenal since. South Africa dismantled its nuclear weapon arsenal. And several countries gave up the nuclear bombs they had.

It is time for all nations with nuclear weapon arsenals to undo them! They can turn to an ADD approach for defense instead (see *Military Defense* description near this chapter's beginning). Countries willing to take down their nuclear arsenals joined by nonproliferation treaty nations should use all peaceful means to persuade unwilling countries to do so. Otherwise, countries opposed to such arsenals should do what they can peacefully to get that action.

A demonstration of this possibility came in 1987 when the US and USSR signed the Intermediate-Range Nuclear Forces Treaty (INF). It removed a whole class of nuclear missiles. Too bad if it's true that modern Russia evaded the treaty by adding nuclear weapons to some conventional missiles. That led to President Trump withdrawing the US from the treaty in 2019. But it is still a good idea if nations involved honor in their treaties and have an effective compliance mechanism in place.

Much the same arguments hold for biological and chemical weapons. There is no need for them with an ADD defense approach.

"Pop" Culture as an Alternative Defense

A *good* war is won with no military combat. Sun Tzu said as much in his ancient Chinese treatise, "The Art of War." Pop culture is a peaceful alternative.

Western popular culture led by the United States has arguably taken over the world! It is not cultural imperialism. And it is not a plot to destroy native mores in other nations as some claim. It stems from voluntary global appeal of food, fashion, film, and music from Earth's most open society, America.

Burgers, jeans, Batman, jazz, and the likes seem to naturally attract the planet's people with few exceptions. This is no surprise given that these pop culture creations result from meshing of diverse tastes. Past open-door immigration policies, combined with free expression and economic choice favored American culture's lead worldwide. Pop culture is simply easy to relate to!

Compare America to countries with authoritarian governments that dictate cultural or religious norms. Commerce in dictatorships of things and ideas is limited to what government officials think best. Ordinary citizens may have other ideas. But they cannot act on them. Governors of despotic nations think the masses must be shielded from *baser instincts* promoted by American popular culture. Government-appointed ministers of culture encourage only *finer arts,* such as nonpolitical poetry, serious painting, and ballet. These *finer arts* are usually best appreciated by persons schooled to enjoy them. Even the least educated American can savor popular films, music, and dance in contrast. Totalitarian nations have little popular culture to offer the world as a consequence. They must be content with appeals to elites. Some of this elitism can be found in America as well to a lesser extent. Think of the Corporation for Public Broadcasting as an example in many of its offerings.

Foreign businesses made inefficient by dependence on government subsidies and protection from competition also fear popular culture. (The same is true in America to a smaller degree.) They are afraid of more efficient corporations born of free enterprise that provide products with mass appeal.

Included are the McDonalds, Coca-Cola, Disney, and the like of American birth.

The strength of popular culture can also be a weakness because of its often universal "lowbrow" appeal. Entertainment it provides can be insulting, negative, sexist, bigoted, and violent among other bad things. But its ease of understanding can unite persons with different languages and cultures. American pop culture, despite flaws, offers human empathy that cannot be matched by totalitarian countries.

America is always in danger of being forced to adopt cultural tastes of government officials in power. That power hopefully will be resisted by the bulk of the US population to preserve individual liberty!

America should try to persuade the world peacefully to adopt its thinking on individual freedom through popular culture. It is more humane than war to accomplish the same goal.

Foreigners Buying in USA Okay

Allowing foreigners that are not enemies to buy US real estate is a good idea!

Such purchases better ensure American security and help its economy without sacrificing American sovereignty. Foreigners with vested interests in US property are inclined to share American concerns for safety and good fortune. They benefit financially only if their property values increase.

A stable, democratic, and rich country made so by free economic choice is their dream.

Sellers of American real estate to foreigners are happy to receive higher prices foreigners often pay. Foreigners tend to pay more for American property than Americans because they usually focus on long-term values. Quick profits are rarely their motive for doing so. American real estate even at high prices is often a better deal than real estate in their own countries. American freedom, security, and stability of governance make the difference.

War with the United States would not be welcome by most foreign US landowners. Property values are best protected by peace and stability. Foreign owners of American real estate are incentivized to become advocates for peace with America in their homeland.

Trade Missions instead of Embassies

Trade missions are more likely than embassies to keep Americans safe! Trade missions paid for and staffed by businesses have an incentive to maintain friendliness with foreigners they trade with. Repeat business is necessary for long-term success. That means being sociable with foreigners' businesses buy from and sell to even if they are unliked. Ditto for foreign buyers of American goods and services. Persons who freely trade are reluctant to war with each other.

Embassies are inherently political in contrast. They focus on the narrow interests of the nation they represent more than the interests of the country they are in. Foreign governments often see embassies as centers for spying on them. Individual citizens of nations with unsavory governments see embassies as giving support to those governments. That could carry over to hatred of the people in the country embassies represent. It makes going to war with those nations easier. And it supports terrorism against the offending country.

Safety of travelers to foreign nations is better assured if no embassy is there to help them. They would think twice about going to a country that might not be safe as a consequence. That is an incentive for nations that depend on foreign tourism to make sure travel there is safe.

Avoid Foreign Civil War Intervention

Civil wars need to be settled without foreign nation intervention if lasting peace is to be achieved. Intervention by America in civil wars in Korea, Vietnam, Afghanistan, and elsewhere failed in unifying those countries. It did lead to more than necessary widespread death, infrastructure ruin, and environmental degradation. And it created a migrant crisis. Recall the second insight mentioned in *Military Defense* near the start of this chapter—absent outside help, countries with the most at stake in conflicts are incentivized to seek peace.

In the 1960s television series *Star Trek*, a spaceship named USS *Enterprise* explored the universe representing the Federation. The Federation included people from planets throughout the cosmos. Its Prime Directive forbade intervening in development of other societies by introducing Earth's political systems, culture, or science. The US, at least in politics, should set an example of individual freedom that speaks for itself. Nations elsewhere can decide voluntarily the kind of society wanted without forcing America's way of life on them. That is the best peaceful way to make friends and influence enemies to adopt American standards for liberty.

Conflict Resolution

Arbitration involves an outside authority deciding on solutions to problems persons or nations are having with each other. All sides are at least satisfied if not completely winners in disputes through conflict resolution. Conflict resolution between nations starts in a neutral location, defines what the conflict is about, focuses on the problem and not those with the problem, lists concerns all sides share instead of differences on the problem, involves listening carefully to all concerns, considers forgiveness, and evaluates self-reform possibilities. Being an effective conflict resolution facilitator requires skill and training that can be learned. Countries seeking peace should include education to create professional conflict resolution facilitators and make use of them. It is better to try conflict resolution first before going to war.

A Worldwide Union of Sovereign Nations

George Orwell in his essay, *The English People*, published at the end of World War II, wrote that the English "have known for 40 years…something that the Russians and the Americans have yet to learn: they know that it is not possible for any one nation to rule the Earth." It applies today to several other countries as well. There, nevertheless, is a need for all countries to work together for the common good of all. It does not take climate change, plant and animal extinction, or a pandemic to prove it. That can confirm it, however.

Albert Einstein and Sigmund Freud wrote a paper in 1933, *Why War?*, stating that the only way to prevent war was to create an international government. Perhaps they had in mind the failure of the Kellogg-Briand Pact of 1928 to bring world peace? The League of Nations founded at the end of World War I did not do any better. And the United Nations, a successor to the League founded in 1945, has failed to bring worldwide peace.

Fear by many world leaders of one-world government has prevented international government from coming about. But it need not be that way. It can be a union of diverse sovereign nations combining their talents and cultures for the common good. That is a reasonable consequence of sharing the Earth and its resources. So, something like a reformed United Nations makes sense and can be enhanced and not destroyed by globalization.

The United Nations has failed to bring worldwide peace because of the same weakness of embassies mentioned earlier; they put narrow self-interests of their country first rather than the common good of all nations if the two conflict. This can be overcome by having representatives of countries who are not primarily conventional politicians.

They should be professional conflict resolution facilitators and cultural anthropologists. It is worth a try!

Incapacitants

It was mentioned under *Military Defense* earlier in this chapter that, "Ideal weapons of war should impede or prevent enemy actions with minimal death, property destruction, pollution, or harm to innocents." Incapacitants that do not kill are among them.

The author of this book took a course on chemical, biological, and radiological warfare in the US Army. He saw a film in it on effects of breathing in some lysergic acid diethylamide (LSD) gas on military performance of soldiers. Trained artillery soldiers laughed uncontrollably and were unable to aim their artillery weapons. A master obstacle course runner was unable to jump from a raised platform or navigate other obstacles. A follow-up on days, weeks, and months later showed no lasting effects or bodily harm. How much more done along these lines since leaving service is unknown to the author because it is classified. But research and perfection of incapacitants like LSD would be a good and humane defense investment. It should be exempted from prohibition of use of chemical weapons. Ditto for sonic and other weapons that only temporarily incapacitate.

The Middle East

Ludwig von Mises, best known as an economist, called the *great irrationalisms* of life—nationalism and religion. This seems to hold true for the Middle East. Peace can come to the Middle East if nationalists and religionists there become more flexible in their demands. Settling land ownership and control peacefully—the major source of conflict—independently of nation boundaries could do it. Take the Israel-Palestinian quarrel as an example.

A fresh approach involves determining area property titles on a case-by-case basis in fair hearings. Successful claimants not occupying their properties would either have the properties returned to them or be compensated in some other way if return is not practical because of existing development or use. It would ideally come from illegal occupiers if restitution could be done with money. Otherwise, money compensation could come voluntarily from persons and countries concerned about ending Middle East discord.

Paying for Defense

A *National Defense Lottery* should be created to help pay for defense. Money won in the lottery should be tax-free as an incentive to buy into it. Lottery money would go into a dedicated Defense Trust Fund used to defray defense costs. A Patriotic Defense Bond should also be created similar to municipal bonds offering tax-free interest. Interest on bonds would be paid by defense contractors proportional to federal funds they receive determined by experts. Bond money would go into the Defense Trust Fund.

> Half the harm that is done in this world is due to people who want to feel important. They don't mean to do harm—but the harm does not interest them. Or they do not see it, or they justify it because they are absorbed in the endless struggle to think well of themselves. (T. S. Eliot 1950)

Crime

There are two kinds of crimes: those committed by people who are caught and convicted, and those committed by people who are not. Which category a particular crime falls into is directly related to the wealth, power, and prestige of the criminal. The former category includes such crimes as purse snatching, mugging, armed robbery, and breaking and entering. The latter category includes war atrocities, embezzlement, most political actions, and budget appropriations.

—Dick Gregory's *Political Primer*, 1972

Crime Penalties

THE PURPOSE OF CRIMINAL LAW SHOULD PRIMARILY be to make those harmed whole again as much as possible. This includes consideration of how victims want their abusers punished. Injury to society is vague at best and should only be a secondary thought.

Focus should be on real criminals that steal from, cheat, and assault innocent people. It should not be on persons who may harm themselves through things like voluntary drug abuse. That is a motivation and education issue.

Crime, Economics, and Minorities

Crime increase because of hard economic times is debatable. It did not happen during the Great Depression of the 1930s despite high unemployment. Linking crime with poor minorities just reflects prejudice.

Restitution to Victims, Heirs, and Assignees

Restitution to victims or heirs and assignees of dead victims should be the main goal of the criminal justice system. Punishment of criminals beyond that should be secondary. Victims or heirs and assignees of dead victims should be able to sue perpetrators in criminal courts for all damages—present and future—as in civil courts. Courts should make awards accordingly.

State-determined punishment independent of considered demands of victims or their heirs and assignees beyond cruel and unusual punishment bans should be ended. Victims or their heirs and assignees should always have a say in what punishment happens to perpetrators. This includes decisions if any on jail time, pardons, forgiveness, or such for convicted criminals.

Defendants or plaintiffs in American courtrooms can now legally be ignored. Judges, lawyers, and "expert" witnesses may decide cases with slight or no input from defendants and plaintiffs. Justice demands more! There should be involvement of defendants and plaintiffs and verdicts from juries of peers if defendants and plaintiffs so elect.

The problem is that American government views the state—not persons hurt—as victim of a crime. Crime for government authorities can be most anything that defies laws of how people behave. But wrongful harm to someone is only a tort—a civil offense—say government officials. You can take somebody to court and sue for damages if that somebody willfully injures you, for example, but the crime is against the state not you in a criminal court. Punishment will be by state laws no matter what non-cruel and unusual redress you ask for. Revenge—if wanted—by seeing offenders jailed or fined (if that) may be all redress you ask for. You may have to suffer abuse on your own with no or scant restitution. Your distress can be overlooked. No one may listen to you or allow you to be listened to in court.

It is time to change the law! Distinctions between criminal crimes and torts should be ended. Persons wrongfully hurt should be able to go to court to seek fullest restitution at all levels. They—not the state—should be recognized as victims of crime unless government property is involved. Both punitive and compensatory demands should be taken into account in courts. Juries should decide issues and make awards rather than court administrators when defendants request it.

Juries Can Rule on Laws

Jurors have the right to vote their conscience while serving on juries. The first US Supreme Court under John Jay confirmed in 1794 that, "The jury has a right to judge both the law as well as the facts in a controversy." Several states codify that right in their state constitutions (Maryland, Oregon, Indiana, and Georgia among them).

It was routine in the past for American judges to inform jurors of this right. Not so much now. No court has dared to deny jury power to acquit despite evidence or law even if relevant discussion is stifled however. This right was reconfirmed in 1972 when the DC Court of Appeals held that a jury has an "unreviewable and irreversible power…to acquit in disregard of the instruction on the law given by the trial judge… The pages of history shine on instances of the jury's exercise of its prerogative to disregard instructions of the judge, for example, acquittals under the fugitive slave law." Other courts have since affirmed the right of veto power by juries.

Make Criminals Pay—Literally—for Crimes

It is only fair that criminals who make the criminal justice system necessary pay for it themselves rather than having public taxpayers do it. Authorities should seek payment directly from convicted felons for all justice system costs—the arrest, the courts, and any jailing. Assets felons have above and beyond justice system costs should be seized to pay their lawful debts, innocent dependent support, and victim restitution as courts dictate. Wealthier felons would pay extra money beyond criminal justice costs into a *felon fund.* This fund would be used to cover unpaid or indigent felons' criminal justice costs. Actuaries under court direction could decide how much should go into the felon fund to at least make it self-supporting. Amounts contributed by felons would be proportional to their financial worth. No public money is called for.

Jailed criminals would have to work to cover any personal jailing cost shortfalls. Prisoners would initially receive spartan but humane accommodations as an incentive to work if they refuse to do so and want more. Better quarters, food, and luxuries could only be bought from money left over from earnings or gifts after expense deductions. Costs for prisoners unable to work because of disabilities would come from the felon fund.

Prisoners could organize businesses behind bars, grow their own food, and work outside of prison under supervision.

They need not be stuck with state-provided jobs at low wage rates. That too could be used as an incentive for more ambitious (better paying) pursuits however.

Responsibility, paying their own way, honest wages, and making restitution would be the focus for convicted felons. That is the positive alternative to a criminal justice system based on punishment. What better way is there to rehabilitate these felons while sparing taxpayers from criminal justice costs?

Gambling

Studies show that state lotteries encourage poor people to gamble on them disproportionally to the general population. Yet independent gambling alternatives that might offer better chances of winning and payoffs are usually illegal. That should come to an end especially when charities can benefit from sponsoring gambling activities.

American-Indians on reservations are allowed to do it for example.

Driving Laws for Teenagers

Driving laws directed only at teenagers invites disrespect for those laws and can be counter-productive to safety. Education about driving safety for all drivers is a better alternative.

Know Your Rights

If you are confronted by the police:

- You never have to speak to police. You *always* have a right to remain silent.
- You can *always* ask if you are being detained. If police are not detaining you, you can *always* leave.
- You should *always* tell police you *do not* consent to a search. Keep in mind that physically interfering with a search may result in *very serious* charges even if you think it is wrongful.
- You should *always* remember the witnesses present during a confrontation with police.

Crime Deterrents

Effective crime deterrents include personal defense, neighborhood watch groups, and independent professional security systems. Police generally respond *after* a crime was committed. Courts have held that government police are not liable in advance for preventing criminal acts. And government police may not respond to calls for help in high-crime dangerous locales.

Overseas Airline Hijackings

Politically-motivated overseas airline hijackings would be reduced if people traveled at their own risk. The US government should not be responsible for risks of overseas travel. Foreign political terrorists and criminals would lose their reason for being hijackers if they could not extort concessions from American government for threatened violence to American citizens. Travelers responsible for their own safety would be more careful in where they travel and how protected they would be. That would be an incentive for airlines, airports, and foreign governments to be more vigilant and creative in how to protect and attract travelers. Economic motivation would be better insurance against airline hijackings than government defense.

Giving Surplus Military Equipment to Police

The US Department of Defense gives surplus military gear to police departments under program loss. It is a bad idea! Dressing police with soldier outfits and arming them with dedicated military weapons can make police think like soldiers. That can lead to overreaction by police in hostile situations, causing needless death and injury. As psychologist, Abraham Maslow, said by analogy, "When the only tool you have is a hammer, you tend to treat everything as nails."

When Governments Promote Hate and Violence

Many government actions promote hate and violence even if unintended. They include some laws that set one standard for adults and another for youths, social security payments that pit young workers against the elderly, minimum wage laws that contribute to unskilled teen and adult unemployment, busing that destroys community school stability, and public housing projects that stigmatize their tenants and invite hostility from neighboring homeowners. All these government actions were meant to solve social problems, but they failed to do so in most cases because of unequal justice under law that catered to counter-productive special interests.

Another culprit is government (public) schools that foster bigotry whether intended or not. Common failure to meet the learning needs of minorities (usually people of color) encourages nonwhite minority hatred of whites. That argues well for school choice and competitive independent schools.

Nonwhite students whose educational needs are not met tend to view themselves *as not as good* as whites. They fail to learn better as a consequence. It tends to foster a false image of themselves as *inferior*. Hatred against more accomplished whites and Asians (also often labeled as persons of color) can be the result.

Government schools commonly excuse nonwhite minorities for not *measuring up*. They pass them along to higher grade levels without the skills required for classroom success. It magnifies their educational deficits and leads to high school dropout rates for them. They look to the streets, maybe with gangs, to feel good about themselves. They may pass this outlook onto their future families so as not to instill a love of school learning.

More public money for schools does not seem to help this situation much.

Competition among government schools and with independent schools may provide answers.

Well-intentioned government-mandated integration that artificially forces persons together who fear or dislike each other can backfire. They may not be sociologically ready for the experience. Mistrust and doubts about *the other* may worsen instead of fostering tolerance and understanding, driving hatred underground. Bigotry motivated beatings, secret Ku Klux Klan cross burnings, swastika graffiti, and other violence are possible consequences. Better to rely on education to encourage voluntary integration.

Busing for integration purposes can also destroy the concept of community. Neighborhood schools have been social stabilization factors historically. Bused children may have less ties to their home neighborhood, viewing it more as just a place to sleep. This *rootlessness* can lead to less respect for home environments and greater likelihood for vandalism there.

Public and government-subsidized housing projects add to the breakdown of sense of *community*. Property renters may find nearby homeowners hostile because of concern about property values (see Chapter 2). The single greatest financial investment for most persons is their home. Concentrations of lower socio-economic groups lured by government housing projects to upper-class neighborhoods may spell trouble. Better to have zoning and building codes that naturally encourage affordable housing (see Chapter 2 again).

Trite but true: the road to hell is paved with good intentions.

More on Government Schools

Ending one-size-fits-all government municipal schools can keep youths in school and away from street crime. Allow people choices between different government or independent schools as already stated. Money parents and caretakers paid in taxes for students can be returned to them and applied by them to schools they think best.

Competition for student money will encourage schools to offer different curriculums to meet individual student needs. Minorities are less likely to be left behind with such a system encouraging them to stay in school. Lousy schools that fail to meet student needs will wither away for lack of money. Good schools that meet student needs will prosper. Competent schools need not fear competition.

Viable alternatives to government schools that meet learning needs of minorities already exist. They include street academies, storefront ghetto schools, cooperatives, home instruction, and more. Educational needs of all could be met by alternative schools now going to failing to near-monopolistic government school systems.

An old American maxim says you cannot trust the foxes to design security fences around hen houses. Governments too often ruled by special interests are unlikely to do what we can do better independently. Bigotry, hatred, violence, and crime can be reduced if not ended by respect for individual rights under just laws.

> Man was born into barbarism when killing his fellow man was a normal condition of existence. He became endowed with a conscience. And he has now reached the day when violence toward another human being must become as abhorrent as eating another's flesh. (Martin Luther King, Jr., *Why We Can't Wait*, 1963)

CHAPTER 6

Education

It is an axiom in political science that unless a people are educated and enlightened it is idle to expect the continuance of civil liberty or the capacity for self-government.

—Texas Declaration of Independence, 1836

EDUCATION HAS BEEN TALKED ABOUT BRIEFLY IN former chapters. This chapter will focus on how government (public) schools should function at elementary and secondary levels and overcome problems. (Government and public-school designation have been used interchangeably because independent schools are also open to the public. Only the term government school will be used in this chapter for utility.)

Get Government and Politics out of Schools

Getting government and politics out of schools would be ideal! Independent schools allow curriculum choice instead of a one-size-fits all politically-dictated government approach. Elected and appointed government officials are less likely to know more about education than teachers, principals, and parents. Independent schools find ways to teach children who for whatever reason fail in government institutionalized schools. What follows are suggestions for improvements in government school education absent replacement by independent schools.

Pare down the number of professional employees between principals and the superintendent of schools. This includes ending jobs for most nonteaching superintendent assistants, behavioral specialists, and "paper pushers" in general. Let parents, teachers, and principals at individual schools create learning objectives for their students within budget. They should enter into written mutually agreed on contracts as to what learning outcomes are called for. Contracts can be assessed each year by all parties involved and adjusted if necessary. Alterations in teaching methodology, and any teacher and principal changes can be made accordingly. How to peacefully arbitrate disputes about contract condition achievements would be included in contracts. Superintendents would be required to abide by and implement arbitration decisions as needed.

Parents should be free to send their children to those schools they think best. Transportation would be the parent's problem, and a measure of their commitment. Working and poor parents without cars can arrange for carpools with neighbors, sharing the expense of having one of them provide transport, safe public transportation, and other means to get their children to schools. Parents can also contract for upgrades in their local school to create a better school in walking distance.

Model High Achievers

Why do some persons or cultural groups—based on skin color or nation of origin—do better in school than others? Whites and Asians do better on average than Blacks and Latinos for example. It certainly is not genetics. More likely are excuses for failure because of past and some current oppression of failing groups. Any fault lies mainly with individual ability and ambition to achieve and family support they get. It would be best to model high achievers than fault them for their success.

Nothing Government Does Is Free

Repeat a falsehood often enough, and people forget it is wrong, and act as if it is true. The word free used by government is a prime example.

Take so-called free public schools. We know that they are paid for indirectly by taxes. But because the taxes are not direct, most people forget that, and act like the schools are free. This makes it easier for special interests to pressure governments to rashly increase school costs by adding non-learning politically-favored activities.

Prudent budgets for public schools can best be achieved by charging for their outlays directly. User fees would encourage parents and guardians of children to pay closer attention to school teaching and costs. Those who cannot afford user fees should get help to do so from other sources.

This argument extends to so-called free government libraries, recreation centers, park facilities, etc.

School Behavior

Behavior troubles in government schools are rooted in compulsory education laws that began in the 1930s. More and more youths ill-suited for the one-size-fits all curriculum in a factory-like classroom setting typical in government schools were forced to be there by law against their will. They behaved badly as a result.

Just as the proverbial squeaky wheel gets the oil, teachers often have to focus on checking rotten behavior at the expense of students there to learn. Few alternatives are given by government for students who do not fit into their traditional classrooms.

Hence the desire of parents for independent schools that might better serve needs of their children who want to learn.

> The fundamental theory of liberty upon which governments in this Union repose excludes any general power of the state to standardize its children by forcing them to accept instruction from public teachers only. The child is not the mere creature of the state; those who nurture him and direct his destiny have the right, coupled with the high duty, to recognize and prepare him for additional obligations. (James Clark McReynolds in a Supreme Court decision, *Pierce v. Society of the Sisters*, 1925)

C H A P T E R   7

Economics and Taxes

If the nation is living within its income, its credit is good.
If in some crisis it lives beyond its income for a year or two
it can usually borrow temporarily on reasonable terms. But
if, like the spendthrift, it throws discretion to the winds,
is willing to make no sacrifice at all in spending, extends
its taxing to the limit of the people's power to pay, and
continues to pile up deficits, it is on the road to bankruptcy.

—Franklin D. Roosevelt (Pittsburgh,
Pennsylvania, October 19, 1932)

ECONOMIST, FRIEDRICH HAYEK, NOTED IN HIS 1944 book, *The Road to Serfdom*, that the market self-adjusts and self-directs itself. Producers tend to produce more when prices rise and consumers tend to consume less and vice versa when prices fall. Freely trading one asset for another is thought to be good by those engaging in such transactions. That is why they do so even if it turns out that they were mistaken in retrospect. Government has a role through democratic institutions to use market-based means to create greater prosperity. It should include protective social provisions along the way for those hurt however.

Government-Provided Services

Federal, state, and county government officials can balance government budgets by adopting fair and progressive public policies. This means limiting governments to doing those things only that people cannot practically do themselves. Military defense, courts, police, and some safety and health actions in the commons are examples. One measure of what governments need not do are services found in telephone business directories.

User Fees

User fees should supplant (not supplement) taxes wherever possible. What can be fairer than having persons who benefit from a government service pay for it? We should all pay for it if all of us benefit from it even if it is called a tax. That is really a user fee by another name. Special provisions should be made to subsidize users who are poor.

User fees for recreation facilities in public nature parks could supplement park protection costs in general. Those parks—US National parks for example—were primarily meant to be enjoyed by persons who love nature and open space. A general fee to cover park maintenance costs as done in US National Parks now can be additional.

User fees lead to more prudent use of government services. Tolls on roads to cover maintenance costs would discourage unnecessary use of them for example. That would lead to less traffic congestion and more use of environmentally friendly mass transit.

Profit Motive

Economics pioneer, Adam Smith, noted that profit motives led to good outcomes because of competition. Sellers of poor-quality goods and services at inflated prices can be undercut by competitors with better deals. It encourages sellers of shoddy goods and services at high prices to be more rational. That means upgrading quality of their goods and services at fairer prices to stay or prosper in business. Governments with monopolies in similar "businesses" face no competition that would spur them to improve. The first-class mail monopoly of the US Postal Service is an example.

Free Markets

Wealthy people have a comparative advantage in gaining political power and using it to further increase their riches. That permits concentration of wealth to a few through government actions they influence. Free markets and competition are checks against such concentration. Free markets work best in societies with stable monetary systems and unbiased courts that enforce voluntary contracts and protect against lawless force and fraud under a uniform set of understandable laws.

Savings and Loan Bank Crisis Prevention

States, such as Maryland, have suffered from a savings and loan bank crisis in the past. How does this happen and how can it be prevented in the future for any state? Here is an explanation:

Picture two kinds of savings and loans. The money of each depositor in one is insured up to $250,000 automatically by the US federal government. It is also allowed to invest its depositor's money as it pleases. The other has no government insurance on deposits. It must obtain the insurance money independently to attract depositors.

Most people deposit money without thought in higher-paying government-insured savings and loans because they feel safe. Government-insured savings and loans have little reason not to engage in riskier investments that promise better returns. They make more money for themselves and depositors than more cautious competitors if they win. Government will bail them out if they lose.

Independent insurers will require that savings and loans they insure make only prudent investments. Protecting themselves from losses is more important than possible better returns from riskier investments. They cannot use tax money to make up for losses or cover deficits unlike governments. Savings and loans independently insured are less likely to have a financial crisis as a consequence.

Miscellaneous Fees for Government Services

Fees for services of government libraries beyond publication and audiovisual material borrowing would be fair. That would include library computer use and copying machines.

Tasteful independently paid for advertisements at transit stops to subsidize bus and train travel should be encouraged. This should include weather-protected bus stops at all stops. That would encourage bus travel as an environmental alternative to auto travel.

Arts and entertainment enterprises should prove that the general public wants them by becoming self-sufficient through fees. Supplemental income should come from independent patronage.

Ads Instead of Taxes to Pay for Public Services

Most public services monopolized by governments can be paid for by ads as well as user fees. Take the US Postal service as an example. Postal losses can be made up by ads on or framed around postage stamps ad fees pay for.

Ads can also be put on government-owned service vehicles. Money raised by such ads would help offset vehicle purchase and maintenance costs. Ads would also lend interest and color to vehicles as they move about.

Tastefully done billboards that do not distract from safe driving should be welcomed. They can provide free pop art for the public as well.

Political Party Subsidies

Political parties should pay their own way rather than be funded at public expense. This includes paying for use of public places for internal purposes, such as conventions, party meetings, and campaigns. They should even cover costs of printing and distributing voting ballots. This was once the case in the USA.

Taxes

Some define money as something that passes from one hand to another on its way to Washington, DC. It is done through taxes!

There is no such thing as a *fair tax* unless it is really a user fee in practice. Any government service should be self-supporting at least through user fees if at all possible. It should be remembered again that special provisions must be made for the truly poor. Such subsidies should not serve as an incentive to remain poor through irresponsible unwholesome living.

Increased taxes in contrast to user fees can make the economy worse! Individuals and businesses tend to organize their lives to avoid taxes. Rising costs of governments are not likely to be offset from falsely expected tax revenue growth consequently.

No word is more misused by governments than the word free. Of course, nothing done by government is free! Taxes pay for it all except for user fees and voluntary support exceptions.

Money taken against your will by force is the normal definition of theft. Not so say government officials when it comes to compulsory taxes. Distinguishing forced taxation from involuntary servitude is not well explained. Government officials claim forced taxes are needed to pay for public services not voluntarily funded. The question is how good is the service if enough people will not fund it voluntarily? It serves special interests mainly if it does not have widespread support.

The healthiest economy is one that pays for itself without taxes. Everything governments do is best when it is at least self-supporting if not profitable. That is the surest way to tell what is a public good and what is not.

Sales Taxes

Expenses for governments hidden in sales taxes force people to pay more than they need to for necessities. That is especially harmful to the poor. People who pay directly for government services they use know what those expenses are. User fee excise taxes are one way to help the needy who cannot afford user fees when possible. Tax credits for voluntary charitable contributions to cover unpaid user fees are another possibility.

Taxes Do Not Always Benefit the General Public

Think about how corrupt government tax systems can be. Governments first take as much tax money as politics allow. A lot of it is siphoned off to pay salaries, perks, and for pet bureaucratic projects of government agencies. Some good for the general public may come from it. But the main aim despite claims to the contrary is to reward special interests that influence elections.

Take charities as an example. Cut out the middle person (governments) and money given directly to charities is maximized. And citizens choose charities they like rather than the ones politicians select that serve their self-interests.

Tax money going to government services themselves cannot be compared to services costs by tax-paying independent enterprises. Independents might cost less and be more efficient despite paying taxes on their services.

Life with Few Taxes

An alternative to most taxes is shifting to a society where citizens pay mainly or exclusively for wanted and used government activities. To do it without chaos means switching from taxes to user fees and lotteries in a progressive manner. It allows independent parties to compete with government in supplying desired services as well.

It starts with a freeze on compulsory new taxes. Governments would have to live within their current income levels. But no government employee would be fired except as usual for cause. Persons now dependent on government patronage for survival without practical substitutes would not suffer cutbacks.

Executive agencies would be phased out other than the military, police, health and safety agencies, and courts needed to protect life, liberty, and property until any alternatives appear. Agency phase-out would be proportional to dropout rates for personnel. Forced unemployment would be avoided by asking personnel from closed agencies to fill positions in remaining agencies vacated by death, retirement, and resignation. Necessary retraining would be provided using money from closed agency budgets. This same money would be used for bonuses and buyouts to spur voluntary exodus from government jobs. Caps on salaries and promotions in agencies headed to termination would further encourage unforced departures.

The tax burden could ultimately be reduced if governments returned to their limited Constitutional functions only. That might allow repeal of income taxes and abolition of the Internal Revenue Service (IRS).

Compensation for Members of Congress

Taxpayers pay a million or more dollars a year for each member of Congress. Costs along with six-figure salaries include office rent and equipment, mailing costs, travel, printing, and other perquisites that can be used in reelection campaigns as well. This is in addition to costs for running Congress as a whole.

Insurance Law Reform

Government insurance laws largely work against affordable insurance. Limits on competition for insurance coverage is an example. Only insurance companies approved and regulated by a state government can sell insurance in that particular state. And the kinds of insurance that can be sold is dictated by a state's law. Most states also prevent insurance agents from discounting their commissions to obtain a sale. These government restrictions force insurance buyers to pay more money than necessary for insurance coverage.

Banks could sell insurance more cheaply because they would not need commissioned sale agents to do so. Most states forbid it.

There is no free market at all in automobile insurance. Minimum government coverage requirements and prescriptions of kinds of insurance allowed restrict cheaper possibilities. Auto insurers compete in trivial ways, making auto insurance more pricey as a consequence.

Costs of liability insurance have skyrocketed thanks to government policies shifting liability from contract law to tort law. Contract law covers voluntary agreements usually declared in writing between sellers and buyers. Tort law deals with matters of possible wrongdoing not covered by seller-buyer contracts. These government policies include expanded rights to sue parties not directly, if at all, at fault. Manufacturers of products get sued for harm from their products caused by failure to follow clear directions and warnings. Providers of service are sued for harm from other services they might never have agreed to supply. Fear of being wrongfully sued frightens product and service providers into buying extra liability insurance. It also discourages innovation that might open up possibilities for new liability.

Bigger payoffs for things they never bargained for leads insurance companies to raise rates and restrict coverage. The end result is less insurance at a higher cost.

Those least able to afford insurance are hurt the most.

Insurance problems and costs would be reduced if insurance could be obtained under true free-market conditions. Novel but honest and practical approaches to insurance coverage should not be stifled by government regulations. Contract law should prevail over tort law when full disclosure, and informed consent are involved in seller-buyer transactions.

Medical Dispute Resolution

Legislative tort reform and stop-loss funds are unfair ways to deal with soaring medical malpractice insurance rates. Doctors should not be shielded from error by governments, and insurance companies should not be publicly subsidized. It's better to have doctors treat patients who voluntarily agree to settle disputes through binding arbitration. That would lower insurance costs without government intervention. It would be a winning situation for doctors, patients, insurance companies, and taxpayers.

Vote by Mail

Voting by mail with safety measures in place to protect against fraud is good economics. No need for polling places. No need to recruit polling place election judges. No need to shut down schools or other government facilities for voting places on primary or election days. No need for rural persons or others to travel to election sites. No state holiday on election day.

Public Financing of Elections

Independent and minor-party candidates need much more money for visibility for election than incumbents with name recognition and an existing constituency. Public financing of elections with equal funding for all candidates disadvantages nonincumbents as a consequence. Think of handicapping in horse racing as an example.

Political Abuse of Statistics

Someone compared statistics to a bikini on a woman: what is revealed is suggestive; what is hidden is vital!

Politicians and special interests wedded to government funding to ensure subsidies use this bikini approach to statistics. Statistics show support and justify government grants and invite more government funding. What is hidden are statistics that suggest the government funding is wasteful or counterproductive. Relatively minor social problems are portrayed as major catastrophes that require quick government action to save the nation. Stress on the worst or emotional part of a statistic can distract attention away from the true situation. This is done by emphasizing the small percent of persons suffering from a problem not directly affecting most.

It should be of concern to all good people if even one person is hurting. But this does not mean government must step in to help at forced government expense. And there is no assurance that government can help in any event. Truly compassionate people promote voluntary social aid and charity. They do not want to be unbenevolent to givers in their quest to be kind to the needy.

Highway Building

Governments should not encourage or subsidize unnecessary automobile travel by highway building (see chapter 2 also). It promotes personal auto travel when more environmentally wholesome mass transit is possible. Mass transit reduces vehicle noise, pollution, and road congestion in residential neighborhoods away from mass transit routes. (Mass transit routes should be located where they provide good access and minimize environmental or residential harm.)

Bicycle Paths

It is only fair that bicycle riders pay for bike paths along roadways. Funding should not come from gasoline or auto mileage taxes meant for roadway building and repair fees. Registration and license fees for bikers that use bike paths can pay for bike path construction and maintenance. A license plate on a bike would also aid traffic enforcement and safety.

Required accident insurance for adult bikers to protect the general public should be considered as well. Neighborhood recreational use of bikes by children is another matter.

Light-Rail Is Risky

Light-rail—aboveground, trolley-like transit—is the latest government-promoted alternative to auto commuting. The problem is that it is expensive to build and run and may not attract enough car commuters to be worthwhile. Only persons with one-track minds would put the public at risk to pay for light-rail.

Any rail system has the weakness of locking people into a particular route. Gone is the flexibility of shifting routes to accommodate new travel patterns. Buses, taxis, and jitneys—vehicles that provide share-ride service—free to set routes and fares are superior.

Governments might better let entrepreneurs, who think light-rail will work, invest in it. They make money while giving citizens a service at no cost to nonusers if they are right. They suffer the loss themselves if they are wrong rather than the public. That is not the case with government-run transit.

Smart persons know that any likely profitable enterprise can find independent investors. Special-interest beneficiaries ask governments to fund risky ventures so that the public shares payment for mistakes. And government-business partnerships favor certain businesses over others whether or not it is best absent competition.

Public Transportation Safety

Persons would be safer from crime on trains and buses with trained armed passengers riding with them. Allowing vetted active and retired police and military people with government safety clearance to carry hidden handguns on transports would help. It comes at no extra public expense. Criminals planning crimes on transports would never be sure they could safely get away with them. That would keep crimes on transports down.

Flying Safely and Cheaply

Flying remains cheaper and safe despite ending government restrictions on air fares and routes in 1983. Airplane flights today cost two-thirds less on average than they did in 1983 adjusted for inflation. Lower flight insurance rates now than in 1983 is further proof that flying deregulation has not affected safety. Deregulation of air travel is not yet complete despite showing it does more good than harm however. Air travel systems are still government owned and operated, and airports government regulated with few exceptions.

Planes take off and land only with consent from federal government-employed air traffic controllers. New runways to accommodate aircraft at airports now crowded because of response to cheaper deregulated fares cannot be built without government approval. Air travel delays are largely the fault of government bureaucracy in management of air traffic control and airports. Independent private owner/operators of air traffic control, free to grow with need, could end bureaucratic obstruction. Ditto for airports. They would be encouraged by competition to act flexibly and imaginatively to provide best service at best prices.

Airlines would be free to operate at off-peak hours by charging higher prices for peak-time flights. Costlier fees for air traffic control at peak times would promote flights at less busy times. Rationed landing slots could be sold to airlines, freeing them to sell them to each other. Airlines with fewer peak-time travelers would then be motivated to sell landing slots to airlines bustling at peak times. That would spread air flights over the day more efficiently. Some airports are already doing this. More liberty from government *red tape* would attract other airports to do the same.

Deregulated airports could impose direct passenger user fees to pay for necessary capacity expansion. Federal law does not allow airports to charge such fees at this time. Billions to build new airports from the Aviation Trust Fund maintained by government taxes on airline tickets goes unused. Few new airports have been built in the USA since 1974 as a consequence. Local zoning laws also prevent construction of smaller airports to relieve larger airports of personal airplane traffic.

> There are those who believe that if you will only legislate to make the well-to-do prosperous, their prosperity will leak through to those below. The Democratic idea, however, has been that if you make the masses prosperous, their prosperity will find its way up through every class which rests upon them. (William Jennings Bryan, Democratic Party National Convention in Chicago, "Cross of Gold" speech, July 8, 1896)

C H A P T E R   8

Science

In recent times, modern science has developed to give mankind, for the first time in the history of the human race, a way of securing a more abundant life which does not simply consist in taking away from someone else.

—Karl Taylor Compton (In a speech before the American Philosophical Society, 1938)

Government Science Research Funding

MAJOR DISCOVERIES IN SCIENCE HAVE HISTORI- cally come mostly by accident or from scientists most people call mavericks. A government official or panel, no matter how constituted to decide on what research to do, would bureaucratize it. The search for objective truth can be compromised by politics as a consequence. Promising but nongovernment sanctioned hypotheses can be overlooked. Scientists with *radical* (not government approved) but perhaps correct notions will not get government funding for their ideas. Deliberate efforts to discover the unforeseeable—original research—is likely impossible. Scientists working in a decentralized manner on their ideas even when peers do not share them historically led to breakthrough discoveries. Recipients of government funding, dependent on same, will be tempted to shape their efforts to assure the funding. Scientific advancement and society can suffer as a result.

Substance Harm Assessment

No one has the right to tangibly hurt an innocent person! Fair and swift justice is the best way to give restitution for and protect from such injury. Government regulation subject to politics and special-interest influence is a more dangerous way.

Health concerns are an example. Courts can stop producers and distributors of things that clearly endanger people forthwith. But governments trying to do the same through regulation can find themselves bogged down in bureaucracy, politics, and challenges. The problem is that governments often try to regulate stuff where ill-health affects are only suspect. And that suspicion is usually grounded in partial truth, popular opinion, or politics instead of scientific fact.

Governments will embrace questionable research that would not stand up in courts when politics demands it. This is chiefly true when cause-and-effect ill-health connections depend on iffy studies of controversial substances. Such is the case when toxicological and epidemiological research is involved.

Toxicological research includes testing effects of certain matter on live animals substituting for people. Similar research directly on people may not be allowed by law, safety, or humane considerations. Public criticism of results is most likely when findings do not confirm popular or special-interest group beliefs. And that criticism may be valid. Dose levels lab animals get are usually much higher than dose levels people normally receive. Ways lab animals are given substances may differ from how people get them as well. People differ enough from other animals to cast doubt on how lab animal findings affect people.

Epidemiological research includes statistical studies of environmental harm on health seen in actual living conditions of people. It shares with toxicological research problems of showing cause-and-effect relationships, but for statistical reasons. Places of living, such as between rural and urban areas, may be too different to properly compare. There are many variables that make it hard to pick on one thing that might make a difference. People also differ greatly in ability to tolerate potentially harmful conditions, such as pollution. That can change with time and age as well. What happens in general may not happen in specific situations to some individuals. Statistical risks and probabilities established for a group may mislead when applied to one person.

An alternative to government health directives when research is uncertain in making those who harm liable for it. Awareness of that liability is an incentive to be extra cautious when you do things that may harm. Nuisance and negligence laws must also be strengthened to allow even the poorest or most sensitive to sue others for legitimate grievances. Courts rather than politics, popular opinion, or special interest groups should decide if harm was done and provide redress if necessary.

Genetic Research and Government

Government regulation of genetic engineering can be unfair, inefficient, and counter-productive although cautionary for public health and safety absent independent safeguards. Torts through an accessible court system might better protect us if potential harm is known in advance.

Of greatest public concern are recombinant DNA experiments where genes of unrelated organisms are snipped out and recombined. There is fear that new and dangerous life forms will be produced by manipulating genetic make-up.

Unfairness comes from government dictates made on the basis of politics rather than real proof. Winners are those who successfully pressure politicians most regardless of merits of their arguments. Findings then depend more on what is likely to ensure politician election than science or public protection.

Political capriciousness is most apparent at so-called public hearings. Testimony is heard and weighed by appointed and elected government officials no matter how unqualified to judge. What is said is not subject to cross-examination by informed citizens or unbiased counsel. There are no strict rules of evidence as in a courtroom.

What a poor way to decide what can be life and death decisions! But it is what happens when controversial concerns are settled through a political hearing process.

Inefficiency of government control of genetic engineering results from determining politically what can or cannot be done experimentally. Science should not be subject to prior political constraints absent court decided clear-and-present danger. Hypotheses—even if politically unpopular—must be tested and checked in a manner scientists can verify.

Scientists chiefly funded by government will likely research along lines government wants. They may not be the best, but scientists have to live too. The search for truth can be compromised as a consequence. Promising but nongovernment sanctioned hypothesis may be overlooked or neglected.

Science in the Public Interest

Science is best when it reflects just the facts—not politics, popular opinion, and grant bias. Truth depends on what good research shows rather than special-interest lobbying and voting by legislators. That is why science in the public interest requires separation between scientific research and government.

Scientific research should first be published in journals where findings can be viewed by other scientists. Any contrary results of other scientists can also be published at the same time or in response. Scientists with doubts can try to copy the research themselves to test for accuracy.

Research is valid when it passes peer review, is uncontested by other research, and can be duplicated. Even then conclusions already reached can be put into question by later research.

Government officials and government grant recipients tend to focus on research that supports what is politically favored in contrast. Traditional methods to measure the quality of research may not be used. Scare tactics are preferred to rally public support for scientifically controversial but emotional vote-getting *problems*. Dubious problems related to climate change and certain chemical cancer warnings are examples.

Contradictory research, even by government's own scientists, may be ignored or squelched if not politically correct. And scientists with unpopular views do not get government funding for their research. Organizations, such as the National Institute of Standards and Technology (NIST) and National Institutes of Health (NIH), would better serve science and the public if free of politics. They could raise money from the public directly if they were independent corporations. Aid can also come from the myriad of corporations that get NIST and NIH information now at public expense.

Science and scientists should not be compromised or corrupted by politics.

Public confidence in scientific findings depend on it.

Research with Animals

Use of live animals other than people in research has become a public issue.

Opponents of such research think that other animals have rights just as people do. But animals other than people only have rights if any given to them by people. Animals cannot tell you what they think even if some people think so. Guesses are usually based on attributing humanlike abilities to those animals known as being anthropomorphic.

People are obligated to cause the least possible pain and suffering for animals that experience some however.

Philosopher, Immanuel Kant, stated that persons are ends in themselves. They are not mere means to ends. (That is one argument against coercive governments as well.) Animal rights philosopher, Tom Regan, thinks Kant's principle applies to animals other than people. But Regan's argument is weak. Neurology denotes other animals, such as highly developed vertebrates, are conscious but not self-conscious as people are. These animals cannot tell good from bad as people can. These animals cannot be moral agents, held responsible for their actions as people should be.

Not able to judge consequences of their behavior, these animals cannot and do not demand rights either. People naturally make choices for those animals. Use of animals other than people for research is no worse than eating or making pets of them. And such research is better than killing dogs and cats at shelters just because they are not adopted.

It is incumbent on people to be humane in animal research, knowing that research can hurt lab animals. Research using live animals should include the three R's—reduction, refinement, and replacement.

Reduction involves use of the fewest live animals in research necessary to get statistically valid results.

Refinement embraces emphasis on research methods that keep injection, maiming, torturing, and general abuse to a minimum.

Replacement means research when feasible with substitutes, such as computers, tissue cultures, unendangered species, and animals that feel less pain.

Government-Subsidized Research Unjust

Supporters of animal rights should not be compelled to subsidize research using live animals right or wrong. But that is what happens when governments use tax money to pay for such research. While still opposed, animal rights advocates would not have to subsidize strictly voluntarily aided research using live animals. That seems fair and respectful of opinions from people who dissent from such research. Hopefully it is returned in kind to the researchers!

Research independently paid for would also reduce political power of animal rights supporters to stop any research. Fair court hearings, instead of special interest politics, would decide rightness or wrongness of research more often. That may not be utopia, but it is more just and rational than deciding things politically.

Evolution Is a Fact

Theory in science is more than just another idea. Scientific theory rests on evidence that can be seen, documented, and verified. Evolution is backed by genetics, embryology, physiology, comparative anatomy, paleontology, and archeology among other sciences. Intelligent design and creationism, in contrast, are based on teleology—rationalizing purpose in nature to fill in blanks in evolution theory that cannot be shown rather than displaying alternatives in a visible way.

Ideas on origins and development of life that are religious based, such as creationism, are possibilities. Because such religious theories are rooted in faith and cannot be scientifically verified, they deserve no time in science classrooms. Moreover, if one speculates on religious-based life development theories, creationism merits no more attention than other life-development, religious theories. These include religious theories of pantheists, polytheists, and others. Creationism is a Christian idea that cannot be proven as scientifically correct.

Food Production

Talking about population outgrowing food production has been going on for at least since political economist, Thomas Robert Malthus, proposed the idea in the early 1800s. It just never happened! Historical trends, showing food output, continues to outpace population growth. More and more food are grown on less and less land with no end in sight. Technology wins.

Third World Farmers

Third World farmers suffer from limited property rights, suppression of farm produce prices by urban politicians wanting abnormally cheap food for city voters, and limited opportunity to get credit for farm expansion. This encourages those farmers to abandon their farms and seek work in urban areas often in affordable shanty towns bordering major cities. That creates pollution and helps spread disease as well as some food production problems. Give full property rights to those farmers, free them from onerous agricultural taxes and subsidy obstacles, and food production aided by science will increase dramatically. Freedom from government expenses for waging war, and enlightened farm political policies will also ensure food abundance. (This last paragraph might have been put in chapters 2 or 7 instead of here absent the science component.)

> The great scientists have been occupied with values—it is only their vulgar followers who think they are not. If scientists like Descartes, Newton, Einstein, Darwin, and Freud don't 'look deeply into experience,' what do they do? They have imaginations as powerful as any poet's and some of them were first rate writers as well. How do you draw the line between <u>Waldon</u> and <u>The Voyage of the Beagle?</u> The product of the scientific imagination is a new vision of relations—like that of artistic imagination. (Edmund Wilson, in a letter to Allen Tate, July 20, 1931, quoted in *Letters on Literature and Politics, 1912–1972,* 1977)

Political Oxymorons

ORCED CHOICE. A FORCED CHOICE IS NOT AN HONest choice at all. Calling a "take it or else" situation a choice when refusal results in severe punishment is especially bogus. An example of the latter was the "choice" given by government to a military draftee. That supposed choice was two years in the Army or five years in prison plus a fine. Similar penalties are offered by the US Internal Revenue Service for persons who choose not to pay taxes. True choices are voluntary.

Compulsory Benevolence. Compelling people against their will to help others is not charity. Charity is charity only when voluntarily given. Such is not the case when government laws and taxes force people to pay for another's welfare no matter how kind that is. What makes matters worse is that charities picked for forced government subsidies are politically determined. That means politically popular, not necessarily most worthy, charities will get the money.

Democratic Socialism. Forceful wealth distribution from each according to ability, to each according to need is undemocratic. Yet, that is the Marxist slogan used by persons who label themselves democratic socialists. Socialism depends on an elite group of government planners with power to tell *society* what to do. Public opposition is checked by government laws. As socialist economist, Robert Heilbroner, wrote, "The creation of socialism requires the curtailment of the central economic freedom of society, namely the right of individuals to own, and therefore to withhold if they wish, the means of production, including their own labor." The bottom line is that socialism requires slavery to the state. It is inherently undemocratic!

Fair Tax. Forcing people to pay taxes for government pursuits they do not want or profit from is unfair. It would be called theft or larceny if anyone other than government did it. Larceny is defined as unlawful taking of property from others without their consent and depriving them of it. Government tax collectors are the only legal crooks (another oxymoron?) in a nation.

Free Government Service. Nothing government does is *free.* Taxes and fees pay for it all. Honesty requires that government services called free be labeled as offered as no extra or direct cost.

Pro-Market Intervention. Government can only support free trade by not intervening in it except to uphold voluntary agreements and contracts. Regulations, tariffs, and quotas not related to public health and safety force consumers to pay more than necessary. Such government intervention is inherently anti-free market and anti-consumer as a consequence.

Entrepreneurs in the Movies

DICTIONARIES DEFINE *ENTREPRENEURS* AS PERSONS who organize, manage, and assume risks of business ventures. But they are more than that. Like them or not, entrepreneurs turn dreams and ideas into products and services that add to what exists and create what is new. Progress would not be possible without them.

Claims have been made that Hollywood has not been kind to entrepreneurs in films. Maybe true in recent years, but not always so. What follows is a sampling of dialogue from major movies that depict entrepreneurs as heroes and innovators.

Two kinds of entrepreneurs are portrayed in the 1962 Cinerama film, *How the West Was Won*. One is Cleve Van Valen (played by Gregory Peck)—a gambler and romantic ready to risk it all to achieve his dreams. He is the maverick entrepreneur often needed to pioneer ventures that others would fear to pursue. In contrast is Mike King (played by Richard Widmark)—the practical, some would say ruthless, entrepreneur who will do whatever it takes to get the job done (building the transcontinental railroad in this case). They reveal their entrepreneurial natures in the following dialogue in the movie:

Van Valen, *while proposing to Lily Prescott (played by Debbie Reynolds)*. "Lily, have you seen San Francisco? It's ugly, and it's small, and it's full of fleas. It burns down almost every five minutes. But each time, they keep rebuilding it a little bigger and a little better than before. It's alive and kickin' and nothin' can stop it. And it makes you want to build something too. A railroad. A steamship line. Somethin' to help the baby grow."

Mike King, *explaining to Army Lieutenant Zeb Hawlings (played by George Peppard) about the railroad breaking its promise to the Arapaho Indians by transporting "buffalo slaughterers" and "settlers" in that were not to arrive in Mike's lifetime.* "All right. It's sooner than I figured. But the railroad's broke. They need the money to keep moving on. No people, no money. No money, no railroad. It's as simple as that…take a look at those people. Half of 'em straight from Europe. They'll have a rough time of it, but they'll make it. And do you know why they'll make it? Because they're willing to change their ways. The Arapahos have to change too. If they don't, they're finished."

Later, after an Arapaho-instigated bison stampede destroys railroad infrastructure and kills railroad workers and their families.

Lt. Rawlings, *looking at a crying child near the child's dead mother, says to Mike King.* "You can live with that?"
Mike King. "I can live with it, or I can die with it…That ain't crying. That's just new life goin' on."

You might call King's futuristic outlook as extreme illustration of economist, Joseph Alois Schumpeter's concept of creative destruction.

A clearer example of what might be called creative destruction is revealed in the 1956 film scripted by Rod Serling, *Patterns*. In it, Bill Briggs (played by Ed Begley), an original executive of thirty years in charge of industrial relations among other things for a formerly small company nurtured into a major corporation by the entrepreneurial skills of the dead business founder's son. Briggs is upset by a plant purchase that would put the plant into receivership for six months idling 900 workers, half the workforce of the village the plant is located in.

Ramsey, *reacting to Brigg's sentimental concern.* "If you would do me the goodness to look at what I consider to be a fairly elementary business principle, by putting 900 men out of work temporarily, we may ultimately employ twice that number in the same town. By cutting production as a result, we will then be able to compete more favorably in the market thus being able to sell more goods. We're not going to ruin the town. We're going to make it, and we save about half-a-million dollars we can put back into the business!"

Ramsey, *recognizing that others see him as callous*. "I'm not looking for gratitude. You can't run a business on thank-you notes…This incredible conception of a huge business being run like a soup kitchen, like a welfare comfort station…This stupid black-and-white idea that honesty and profitability are incompatible. I just happen to feel that the atmosphere of a huge company cannot be cathedralized."

Ramsey, *lecturing Fred Staples (played by Van Heflin) brought into the company to replace Briggs while he was alive following Briggs's fatal heart attack about the business*. "It's no one's business. It belongs only to the best, to those who can control it, sustain it, nurture it, keep it going. Right now, it belongs to us because we're producing. But in the future, it belongs to whoever has the brains, the nerve, the skill to take it away from us."

What many would consider a more benign and affirmative entrepreneurial attitude is depicted in the 1954 film, *Sabrina* (remade in 1995). In the original movie, Linus Larabee (played by Humphrey Bogart) is the successful multi-millionaire head of Larabee Industries, an international multiproduct company headquartered in New York City. His less-business-inclined playboy brother, David (played by William Holden) questions Linus as to why Linus continues to work for the company producing new products when Linus has "all the money in the world."

Linus. "What's money got to do with it? If making money was all there was, it'd hardly be worthwhile going into the office. Money is a by-product."

Further questioning Linus about a new, resilient, bulletproof plastic, Linus developed that "doesn't burn, doesn't torch, doesn't melt, tastes sweet, and is made of sugar cane" intended for manufacture in a third-world country.

David, *comments*. "You're going into plastics now. What would that prove?"
Linus, *retorts*. "Prove? Nothing much. A new product has been found, something of use to the world. So, a new industry moves into an undeveloped area. Factories go up, machines are brought in, a harbor is dug, and you're in business. It's purely coincidental that people who never had a dime suddenly have a dollar, and barefooted kids wear shoes and have their teeth fixed and faces washed. What's wrong with the urge that gives people libraries,

hospitals, baseball diamonds, and movies on a Saturday night?"

Peter Bailey (played by Samuel S. Hind), the chief entre-preneur behind the Building and Loan in Frank Capra's 1946 film, *It's a Wonderful Life*, expressing another benevolent if humbler concept than Linus's when trying to convince his son, George (played by James Stewart) to stay in the business.

Peter Bailey. "You know, George, I feel that in a small way we're doing something important, satisfying a funda-mental urge. It's deep in the race of man to want his own roof and walls and fireplace. And we're helping him to get those things in our shabby little office."

Extending his dad's thoughts after his father dies in response to Building and Loan director, Henry F. Potter (played by Lionel Barrymore) who wants to shut down the business because it competes with his bank with the excuse that "easy" loans the Building and Loan gave, created *"a dis-contented, lazy rabble instead of a thrifty working class."*

George, *lecturing Potter about his dad.* "He did help a few peo-ple get out of your slums, Mr. Potter. And what's wrong with that? Doesn't it make them better citizens, and doesn't it make them better customers? You said that… what'd you say a minute ago? They had to wait and save their money before they even thought of a decent home. Wait? Wait for what? Until their children grow up and leave them? Until they're so old and broken-down that they…Do you know how long it takes a working man to save $5,000? Just remember this, Mr. Potter, that this rabble you're talking about, they do most of the working and paying and living and dying in this community. Well, is it too much to have them work and pay and live and die in a couple of decent rooms and a bath?"

In the 1988 film, *Tucker: The Man and His Dream*, based on the life of entrepreneur Preston Tucker, who developed the sleek, safety-featured Tucker car inaugurated June 1947 in Chicago, we learn how business can use government to stifle competition. Most auto companies kept a conventional look for their cars to save money rather than retool after World War II. Tucker cars, in contrast, included individual wheel suspension, safety chambers, interchangeable high-and-cushioned front and back seats, safety belts (a first), under-seat heaters, pop-out safety glass wind-shields (a first), fuel injection, a 166-horsepower rear engine capable of 130 mph speed (a first) that got twenty miles to the gallon of gasoline despite its big (for the time) 130-inch wheel base, and other features, such as the "Cyclops" center-front light.

The "Big Three" auto companies probably could not have stopped Tucker cars from competing with them without federal government help. Their actions reinforced what

Tucker (played by Jeff Bridges in the movie) already thought when he responds to his son's desire to work with him rather than go to college.

Tucker. "As far as I'm concerned, the two crummiest things a person can be are lawyers and politicians."

Tucker later tells his adversary, Senator Ferguson (played by Jeff's real-life dad, Lloyd Bridges) who refuses to shake Tucker's hand by putting his hands in his own pants' pockets.

Tucker. "That's something I never thought I'd live to see. A politician with his hands in his own pockets."

In his summary defense before a jury at his trial instigated on false charges by the "Big Three" auto companies and the government, Tucker states his case for entrepreneurial innovation not hampered by government.

Tucker. "When I was a boy, I used to read all about Edison and the Wright Brothers and Mr. Ford. They were my heroes. Rags to riches, that's not the name of a book. That's what this country is all about. We invented the free enterprise system where everybody no matter who he was, where he came from, what class he belonged to, if he came up with a better idea about anything, there was no limit to how far he could go. I grew up a generation too late, I guess, because now the way the system works, the loner, the dreamer, the crackpot who comes up with some crazy idea that everybody laughs at, that later turns out to revolutionize the world, he's squashed from above before he's heard or gets to do it. The bureaucrats would rather kill a new idea than let it rock the boat. If Benjamin Franklin were alive today, he'd be put in jail for experimenting with lightning without a permit. It's true! We're all puffed up with ourselves now because we invented the bomb, dropped it, beat the daylights out of the Japanese and Nazis…But if big business closes the door on the little guy with a new idea, we're not only closing the door on progress, and sabotaging everything we fought for, everything the country stands for…But one day we're going to find ourselves at the bottom of the heap instead of king of the hill having no idea how we got there, buying radios and cars from our former enemies. I don't believe that's going to happen. I can't believe it because if I ever stop believing in plain old common horse sense of the American people, no way could I get out of bed in the morning."

It is a tribute to Americans at the time that Tucker was found *not guilty*. One wonders if ordinary citizens today would understand the value of free enterprise to reach the same verdict on a jury in a similar case.

Business entrepreneurial guidance is the theme of the 1953 film, *Executive Suite.* Following the death of Avery Bullard (never seen in the movie), who headed up the Tredway Furniture Company, a new president has to be chosen from company vice-presidents who also served on the company's board of directors. Comptroller and accountant, Loren Shaw (played by Frederic March), is a likely candidate for company president.

Comptrollers and accountants were arguably in the forefront of thinking about who could best lead businesses by the 1950s rather than the Preston Tucker dreamer types. But the idea of quality being important for ultimate success rather than short-term profits alone leads to Donald Walling (played by William Holden) who oversees design of the company's furniture being selected as company president. He wins his coming-from-behind election with his spirited confrontation with Shaw before the other directors.

Shaw. "Efficiency has become a dirty word. Budget control has a bad odor. Well, that's my job. That's my responsibility. To plug every profit leak. To run to earth every single case of waste and inefficiency in this company. If I have to step on toes and hurt feelings in the process, that can't be helped. But nobody's going to say I ever had anything but the best interests of this company at heart while I was doing it. You take a look at the record for the past three years. Fight that record, my record."

Walling. "In other words, Bullard was the right kind of man to save this company from disaster to build it up and set it on its way. But now we need a different kind of management, one that will dedicate itself to paying the maximum dividends to stockholders. Is that it?"

Shaw. "I don't know if I'd express it in those words, but, yes, that's substantially what I do mean."

Walling. "Shaw, let me ask you something. The president of a company like Tredway would have to be a man of outstanding qualities, wouldn't he?" A man prepared to make many personal sacrifices, willing to devote himself to the company, mind and heart, body and soul."

Shaw. "Naturally."

Walling. "Why? Why would he do it? What would be his incentive?"

Shaw. "Outside of salary, there's such a thing as success. The sense of accomplishment."

Walling. "Exactly! Now, let's assume, Shaw, that you're the man running the Tredway company your way. Would you be satisfied to measure your life's work by how much you raised the dividend? Would you regard your life as a success? Just because you managed to get the dividend to $3 or $4 or five or six or seven? Would that be enough? Is that what you want engraved on your tombstone when you die—the dividend record of the Tredway company?"

Shaw. "Are you suggesting that earnings aren't important?"

Walling. "I'm suggesting no such thing, and you know it! Shaw's right that we have an obligation to our shareholders. But it's a bigger obligation than raising the dividend. We have an obligation to keep this company alive, not just this year, or next, or the year after that. Sometimes you have to use your profits for the growth of the company, not pay them all out in dividends to impress the stockholders with your management record. There's your waste, Shaw! There's your inefficiency! Stop growing and you die! Turn your back on experimentation and planning for tomorrow because they don't contribute to dividends today and you won't have tomorrow because there won't be a company…Grabbing for the quick and easy thing, that's just a lack of faith in the future, something that's in the air today, the grasping of a lot of men who know they lost their faith, but aren't sure what it is, or how they happened to lose it. Avery Bullard was one of them. He'd been so busy building a great production machine that he finally lost sight of why he was building it, or why he was the man he was (if he ever really knew)."

Following comments by Mrs. Avery Bullard (played by Barbara Stanwyck) and Jesse Q. Grimm (played by Dean Jagger), both company directors.

Walling, *continuing*. "The force behind a great company has to be more than the pride of one man. It has to be the pride of thousands. You can't make men work for money alone. You starve their souls when you try it. And you can starve a company to death in the same way. Avery Bullard must have known that once. But he became lost these last few years. The company had been saved. There were no more battles to win. Now he had to find something to feed his pride—bigger sales, more profit, something. And that's when we started this: the K-F line (of furniture)."

Josiah Walter Dudley (played by Paul Douglas), *Walling then directs a question to the sales director*. "Walt, are your boys proud when they go out and sell this stuff (the K-F line) when they know the finish is gonna crack, the veneer will split off, and the legs come loose?"

Shaw, *coming in again*. "Wait a minute! That's price merchandise. It serves a purpose. In the profit structure of this company, we're not cheating anybody."

Walling. "Ourselves."

Shaw, *retorting*. "At that price, the customer knows exactly what he's going to get."

Walling, *smashing a chair from the K-F line and saying*. "This is what Tredway has come to mean. And what do you suppose the people think of us when they buy it? How do you suppose the men in the factories feel when they make it? What must they think of a management that's willing to stoop to selling this kind of junk in order to add a dime a year to dividends? Do you know there are men who've refused to work on the K-F line? Who've taken a $7.50-a-week cut to get transferred to something else?"

Shaw. "Well, after all, that's only part of the business. Eventually we can cut down on the line."

Walling. "We'll drop that line! And we'll never ask a man to do anything that will poison his pride in himself or his work. We'll have a line of low-price furniture. A new and different line, as different from anything we're making today as a modern automobile is different than a covered wagon. That's what you want Walt, isn't it? What you've always wanted? Merchandise that will sell because it has beauty and function and value, not because the buyers like your Scotch or think you're a good egg. The kind of stuff that you, Jesse, will be able to feel in your guts when you know it's coming off your production line. A product that you will be able to budget to the nearest hundredth of a cent, Shaw, because it will be scientifically and efficiently designed. And something you'll be proud to have your name on, Mrs. Tredway. We're going to get the people what they need at prices they can afford to pay. And as fresh needs come up, we'll satisfy them, too, with something new and even more exciting. And when we achieve that, we'll really start to grow! We're not gonna die. We're gonna live! And it's going to take every bit of business and creative energy in this company from the mills and factories right to the top of the Tower (the top floor of the company's headquarters building). And we're going to do it together. Every one of us. Right here at Tredway."

Most popularly misunderstood in a film was Gordon Gekko (played by Michael Douglas) who was the take-over entrepreneur in the 1985 movie, *Wall Street*. His chief crime in the film was intelligence collecting considered illegal under government laws, but not a crime per se in other circumstances, such as war. He is often misquoted as saying "greed is good" when the actual statement was "greed—for lack of a better word—is good." In reality, the speech that quote was included in the movie at the annual meeting of the Teldar Paper Company reflects the positive nature of take-over entrepreneurs.

Gordon Gekko. "Well, ladies and gentlemen, I'm not going to indulge in fantasies, but in political and economic reality. America has become a second-rate power. It's trade deficit and its fiscal deficit are at nightmare proportions. Now in the days of the free market, when our country was a top industrial power, there was accountability to the stockholder. The Carnegies, the Mellons, the men that built this great industrial empire, made sure it was their money at stake. Today, management has no stake in the company. And where does Mr. Cromwell (Teldar's CEO) put his million-dollar salary? Not in Teldar stock.

He owns less than one percent. You (stockholders) own the company. That's right! You, the stockholder. And you are all being royally screwed over by these bureaucrats (company officials) with their steak luncheons, their hunting and fishing trips, their corporate jets, and golden parachutes. Teldar Paper has thirty-three different vice-presidents each, earning over $200,000 a year. Now I've spent the last two months analyzing what all these guys do, and I still can't figure it out. One thing I do know is that our paper company lost $110 million last year. And I'll bet half of that was spent on all the paperwork, going back and forth between all these vice-presidents. The new law of evolution in corporate America seems to be survival of the unfittest. Well, in my book, you either do it right or you get eliminated. In the last seven deals that I have been involved with, there were 2.5 million stockholders who have made a pretax profit of $12 billion…I am not a destroyer of companies. I am a liberator of them! The point is, ladies and gentlemen, that greed—for lack of a better word—is good. Greed is right. Greed works. Greed clarifies—cuts through and captures the essence of the evolutionary spirit. Greed, in all its forms—greed for life, for money, for love, and for knowledge—has marked the upward surge of mankind. And greed—you mark my words—will not only save Teldar Paper, but that other malfunctioning corporation called the USA."

Perhaps the most unusual example of an entrepreneur in a film is Corporal King (played by George Segal) in the 1965 movie, *King Rat*, based on James Clavell's novel about an entrepreneur (King) in the infamous Chiangi Japanese prisoner-of-war camp in Singapore during World War II. King is among the few Americans mixed in with English and Australian war prisoners. His ability to thrive under terrible camp conditions by *wheeling and dealing* acts like Adam Smith's "invisible hand" to keep many others alive even if they do not understand or appreciate it. His entourage that performs personal services for him hate doing so even though they live better than others in the camp because of King.

One person who understands the value of King is an English soldier, Peter Marlowe (played by James Fox). Marlowe was recruited by King to help because of his knowledge of Malay and Japanese languages useful to King for negotiations. In defending King in dialogue with English lieutenant, Robin Grey (played by Tom Courtney), who enforces law in the camp and hates King for his manipulations, Marlowe says to King, "King is a friend. He's not a crook, and he's not a thief."

Grey responds, "But he's a liar."

Marlowe retorts, "We're all liars, Grey. You gotta be a liar (here) to stay alive. You do a lot of things to stay alive."

When the camp is freed by the English army, and King leaves camp by truck suspect because he looks so good physically compared to all other prisoners, officers and enlisted men alike, Grey says to Marlowe, "That was worth waiting for. Seeing him (King) cut down to size like that. It's our turn now, Marlowe. Still, you can be proud you were his friend, I suppose."

Marlowe responds, "It wouldn't occur to you you're alive because of what he gave you."

Grey asks, "What are you talking about? I never took anything from him. He never gave me anything."

Marlowe answers, "Only hate, Grey, only hate."

Hate gave Grey a purpose for living, generally thought critical for surviving, and another way the "invisible hand" might work for the better.

There are other films about entrepreneurs probably worth quoting. Keep searching for them.

GERALD SCHNEIDER IS AN environmental educational consultant who, among other things, served as the first executive director of the Audubon Naturalist Society (now called Nature Forward) in Chevy Chase, Maryland. He also wrote a *Libertarian outlook* political column for four Montgomery County, Maryland, newspapers for eleven years labeled "Gerry's Judgments" in its final years. Gerald sees all the world's problems as an environmental concern in need of rational and ethical solutions.

www.ingramcontent.com/pod-product-compliance
Lightning Source LLC
Chambersburg PA
CBHW051448250726
48655CB00001B/307